CELEBRATE
THE
CHRISTIAN STORY

Also by Michael Perham and published by SPCK:
Liturgy Pastoral and Parochial
Lively Sacrifice
Waiting for the Risen Christ
Welcoming the Light of Christ

As editor:
Towards Liturgy 2000
Enriching the Christian Year
(published in association with the Alcuin Club)
The renewal of Common Prayer
(published jointly with Church House Publishing)

CELEBRATE
THE
CHRISTIAN STORY

*An introduction to the New Calendar,
Lectionary and Collects of the Church of
England*

MICHAEL PERHAM

First published 1997
SPCK
Holy Trinity Church
Marylebone Road
London NW1 4DU

British Library Cataloguing in Publication Data

A catalogue record for this book is available from the British Library.

ISBN 0–281–05107–0

Typeset by Pioneer Associates, Perthshire
Printed in Great Britain by
Biddles Ltd, Guildford and King's Lynn

For Rachel, Anna, Sarah and Mary,
with love and with the hope they may share
something of their father's delight in the
Christian year

Contents

Preface

It is the privilege of the Church to celebrate the Christian story and to invite others to share in doing so. It is more than reading the Scriptures from week to week. It is placing that reading within the liturgical context of the Christian year, of prayer and of worship. In the last few years it has been my particular privilege, with colleagues in the Liturgical Commission and the Inter-Provincial Group, to work on the revision of the Church of England's own way of celebrating the Christian story in its new calendar, lectionary and collects. In this book I have tried to share some of the thinking of that revision process and to introduce the new authorized material in such a way that people will understand its principles and its provisions readily and begin to use it with a real sense of anticipation and excitement.

I have not told in any detail the story of the development of the Christian year over the centuries, though inevitably some of that does feature. For more of the historical background and much more in relation to the seasons of the year, I refer readers to two books that Bishop Kenneth Stevenson and I wrote together as commentaries on earlier Church of England provision. *Waiting for the Risen Christ* (SPCK, 1986) introduces *Lent, Holy Week and Easter* (SPCK/CHP, 1995); *Welcoming the Light of Christ* (SPCK, 1991) introduces *The Promise of His Glory* (Mowbray/CHP, 1991).

The material in this book is newly written, except that chapter 2, Lectionary, is a revised form of a lecture given

Preface

in June 1996 to a PRAXIS Liturgical Day and then circulated to all PRAXIS members two months later.

I owe a great deal to my colleagues on the Liturgical Commission who worked closest with me on the calendar, lectionary and collect proposals. They were Canon Jane Sinclair, Canon John Sweet and Brother Tristam SSF. I am grateful for their wisdom, hard work and friendship. I have also been helped by the clergy and congregation of Norwich Cathedral, where I minister, who lived patiently with many of the new provisions while they were still proposals or sometimes not much more than ideas. I remain grateful to my publishers, SPCK, and in particular to Rachel Boulding, who is always encouraging and understanding of the constraints under which writing is often done. To all of these and to my wife Alison, for her support and forbearance, I express my warmest thanks.

Michael Perham

1

Season, word and prayer

INTRODUCTION

Season, word and prayer belong together. It is the calendar of the Christian year that gives shape to the lectionary. It is also the calendar that gives the seasonal emphasis to the collect of a particular day. The relationship of calendar, lectionary and collect – season, word and prayer – is an important but subtle one. Where the three come together successfully, Christian people are given an effective way of entry into the celebration and exploration of the 'mystery of faith'. That celebration and exploration, at the same time stimulating and satisfying, can enrich their Christian discipleship. The Church of England's new *Calendar, Lectionary and Collects* sets out to be just that sort of way in to Christian faith and practice. 'Calendar, Lectionary and Collects' does not sound exciting, perhaps not even important, but it turns out to be much more than a convenient way of ensuring that Christian festivals and Bible passages are not neglected; it is a way into the heart of things. To keep in step with the seasons of the Christian year, using its Scripture readings and its prayer, is a journey of the spirit.

The new provision, *Calendar, Lectionary and Collects for the Year 2000*, will be referred to in this book as CLC 2000. The year 2000 is attached to it because in that year it is intended to replace the present calendar, lectionary and collects in *The Alternative Service Book 1980*. A new service book or series of service books will replace

1

the ASB and the authorization for it is likely to be withdrawn. However CLC 2000 has been authorized for use, alongside existing provision, from The First Sunday of Advent 1997, so churches and parishes that choose to will be able to use its three-year cycle right through before the new book supplants the ASB three years later.

But why a new round of liturgical change after only twenty years? Obviously that is a complex question with a variety of answers. But it needs to be remembered that the Church of England embarked in the 1960s on the most far-reaching liturgical changes since the sixteenth century. It is not surprising that, while some of the reforms introduced then have won general approval and established themselves securely in only a generation, others have not stood the test even of a short time. In the sixteenth century there was period during which there were successive changes. The twentieth century is different. We have not lived through the kind of political and religious changes of direction that marked the reigns of Henry VIII, Edward VI, Mary and Elizabeth, and which were partly responsible for the changes to the liturgy, but we have lived through enormous cultural changes and it is possible to discern that the liturgical revisions of the 1960 and 1970s reflect a cultural fashion that has dated quickly. One only has to look at the world of architecture and buildings to see what one generation regards as innovative, exciting and catching the spirit of the age can, only a few year's later, seem transitory and tired.

As we move into a new century, there is a greater willingness to reverence the past and to value the heritage, than there was a generation ago.

There is also in the Church, some evidence of a greater desire to relate to the wider community, to be in dialogue with 'folk religion', and to build bridges, compared to twenty-five years ago. There is also a clearer vision of the need for a Church that gives evangelism priority and that provides worship that serves that priority. In brief, it is a strangely different world from the one in which our new services were devised only a generation ago. That is in itself a warning against imagining that every age can make all things new in liturgy in a way that can last, and, unless we want to live with constant change, that argues for a liturgy that evolves slowly rather than one that changes rapidly. But it does not remove from the present generation the responsibility to create the best liturgy it can for the years ahead.

Although there are others, I detect three major pressures for the revision of *The Alternative Service Book.* The first concerns commonality. The second is a series of related questions about language. The third is about particular parts of the ASB provision that have given least satisfaction.

COMMON PRAYER

The issue of commonality is one that has come to the fore in the 1990s, not least through the publication in 1993 of a series of essays by the Church of England Liturgical Commission entitled *The Renewal of Common Prayer* (Church House Publishing and SPCK), though there had been some people patiently raising the issue through the previous twenty years and often finding themselves speaking as voices in the wilderness. The issue at its most simple is this. How much freedom, variety and local decision making in liturgy can there be without the sacrifice of 'common prayer', that sense (and experience) that, wherever you go in England and whenever you go to church, there is a sense of the familiar that helps to form the Church, its belief, its cohesion and the sanctity of its members?

There are some who deeply regret the passing of the kind of uniformity that *The Book of Common Prayer* imposed until the 1960s. It was not a total uniformity, for every church had its style, but, in general, particularly in terms of text, you knew where you were, you knew quite a lot by heart if you were a regular churchgoer, and, though you took your Prayer Book with you to church, you hardly needed to open it, for you knew what would be done and said. But those who deeply regret the passing of that degree of uniformity are probably a minority, and most church people consider themselves to have been enriched by the freedom that new services have brought. This has been the freedom to vary, to be spontaneous, to take seriously the need of a particular congregation, to draw on a variety of sources, to be adventurous. Most church people do not wish to see that new world disappear. So the question is not so much about a return to uniformity, but in knowing where to set limits for the sake of common prayer. We are not all agreed on this and, behind some of the debates about particular service forms, there often lies a more philosophical debate about the degree of common prayer on to which we believe we have to hold. For common prayer does defend our doctrine (and, in particular, the doctrinal stance of the Church of England), it contributes enormously to the cohesion of a Church that relies on a sense of belonging to hold it together, and it forms people in their Christian spirituality by giving them words of Scripture and prayer that they hear in the liturgy but make their own in the ups and downs of daily living. A new service book will want to renegotiate the relationship between common prayer and liturgical diversity, not least in relation to the Christian year and the reading of the Scriptures through it.

LITURGICAL LANGUAGE

The second major pressure for the revision of the ASB is a series of issues related to language. The first is a plea, very different from the plea – in the 1960s to leave behind the language of the Prayer Book – to introduce liturgical language that is poetic, rhythmic, resonant and memorable. In general, people are not asking for a return to older forms, but for texts that are thoroughly contemporary, with intelligibility still high on the agenda, and a desire often for language more pictorial than technical, yet, among all these concerns, richer and more satisfying, more likely to find a way into the memory and the soul. It is a tall order and the creation of a new liturgical rhetoric, which cannot be contrived and has to emerge naturally, probably through the trial and error of the wordsmiths, is a slow business. But there has been movement and progress since the services that found their way into the ASB were being devised. A revision now can reflect this new approach.

Linked with that central question of liturgical language are other related ones that cannot be much more than listed here.

1. Is there a place in contemporary liturgy for some ancient texts, including texts from *The Book of Common Prayer*, used as they stand without any attempt to modernize them? The answer in the Liturgical Commission and in the Synod is a clearer 'Yes' to this than was the case twenty-five years ago.
2. Is the Church of England still committed to using international and ecumenical texts or forms wherever

these exist, or is it prepared, for the sake of texts more rooted in our own history and reflecting our own contemporary cultural attitudes, prepared to go it alone? In general the answer seems to be that the Church of England is so committed, but not in so resolute a manner that exceptions cannot be made. The application of this to the calendar of the Christian year or an ecumenical lectionary is obviously important.

3. Where does the Church of England stand on the issue of gender-inclusive language? Here there is no consensus. Some in the Church of England see the whole issue as one of 'political correctness' and passing fashion, and would see no changes at all to liturgical texts. Others would welcome some modest changes that reflect a culture in which 'man' and 'men' do not seem to be words that affirm women, even if they include them. Yet others would go further and look to see whether the language we use of God need speak so determinedly of the deity as 'he' and use so much male language of One who is beyond gender. To write liturgy when these questions divide church people so fundamentally is difficult. The position the Liturgical Commission has adopted, with the synod's approval, is to be wary of changing ancient texts, to modify contemporary forms in relation to the way we speak of human beings, to be particularly careful to preserve theological precision in speaking of the incarnation, and to go for modifications in the way we speak of God only when international texts lead us down that path (and not always then).

All these questions of language are important when considering the provision of collects, many of which are deeply established in the memory of church people, but which raise exactly the problems posed in these paragraphs.

THE NEED FOR NEW RITES

The third and final major pressure for change has been the fact that some parts of the ASB have seemed particularly unsatisfactory; some parts have emerged strongly from a generation of use, not least the revised eucharistic rite. The Funeral Service has never seemed satisfactory. The orders for Morning and Evening Prayer have nearly always seemed a wasted opportunity. The lectionary, and therefore the calendar that to some extent was made to fits its presuppositions, and the collects that reflected its themes, have worn thin.

THE MOVE TOWARDS REVISION

These then have been among the principle pressures to replace the ASB in the year 2000. Once that decision had been taken (and it was not one that many have opposed), it was natural that the calendar, lectionary and collect provision should be the first material brought forward for revision, not only because it had emerged as one of the areas of dissatisfaction, but also because one cannot begin to revise the various rites, with their need to reflect the seasons, until one has the calendar in place. 'What is the shape of the Christian year?' is almost the first question to be faced in a process of liturgical renewal.

This was the first question the Liturgical Commission faced. It appointed a group of four of its members to work on the provisions. Two of them also began work in a wider group, that has come to be known as the

'Inter-Provincial Group', in which representatives of the Church of Ireland, the Church in Wales and the Scottish Episcopal Church joined with the Church of England in trying to find a way forward in which all four churches could share. The Inter-Provincial Group looked at questions of calendar and lectionary, to try to keep in step, but the major part of its work was in producing the collects and post-communion prayers for Sundays and Holy Days. Although it will take time for the governing bodies of all four churches to ratify these proposals, it seems that all the Anglican churches in the British Isles will soon be using almost identical provisions.

Although it was the prayers that occupied most of the Inter-Provincial Group's time, it did begin with the calendar. Despite the fact that there was, from the start, a strong lectionary contender, there was a determination that the process must begin with the Christian year. To do otherwise would be to put the cart before the horse. The first need is to establish the shape and pattern of the Christian year. Only after that can one move on to find Scripture readings and prayers to enrich the celebration of the seasons.

The proposals from the Liturgical Commission's Group and from the Inter-Provincial Group underwent full discussion and some amendment in both the full Commission and the House of Bishops before being published (as GS 1161) in June 1995 and brought in the following month to the General Synod, where they were warmly received and referred to a Revision Committee of the Synod. That committee, meeting under the chairmanship of the Bishop of Sheffield, received a large number of proposals, but what emerged a year later (as GS 1161A) did not alter the original proposals in any fundamental way, though there were a large number of changes, not least in the calendar of 'saints'. In July 1996 the Synod gave approval to the Revision Committee's report and declined to refer any issues back to the committee for reconsideration. At the November 1996 Synod the proposals were given Final Approval, with only six votes in the entire Synod against.

FIVE PRINCIPLES OF CLC 2000

There are five basic principles that lay behind CLC 2000. The first of these was to be 'in step'. The Church of England did not want to go out on a limb. But the difficulty was in knowing with whom to be in step, and here there were at least three contenders.

In step with the Prayer Book

The first was *The Book of Common Prayer*. The Prayer Book remains the primary worship book of the Church of England, as well as a doctrinal norm, and Anglicans ought to depart from its provisions only where there is a clear need. Although not everyone will agree, most Anglicans have accepted that there is a need to provide an alternative to its sixteenth and seventeenth century language. But is there a need to depart from it in terms of calendar and, even if collects have to be in two versions, to allow for traditional and contemporary language forms, can they not still be two versions of the same prayer? At a practical level, is the Church well served if, for most Sundays of the year, it has two different Sunday titles depending which service book is being used? Being in step with the Prayer Book where possible became one of the Commission's aims.

9

In step with others

But equally there was a desire to be in step with the present day usage of other churches, and in particular with the Roman Catholic Church, with which Anglicans share a strong common liturgical tradition. The rigorous way in which the liturgy of that Church has been revised since the Second Vatican Council has very often shown to other churches the way forward (or, sometimes, the way back to very ancient practice) and Anglicans, in particular, have been ready to learn from the considerable liturgical scholarship of the Church of Rome. To be in step to a greater extent with the Roman Catholic Church in matters of calendar and lectionary seemed a proper objective. But, of course, such an aim was sometimes in conflict with the desire to be in step with *The Book of Common Prayer*.

A third element was the wish to be in step with the wider Anglican world, some of which has followed ASB provision, other parts of which have gone a different way, often closer to the Roman way. In particular there was the desire already mentioned to try to keep the Anglican churches in the British Isles in step. This pan-Anglican or inter-provincial element further complicated the picture, so that what looks like a simple principle to be in step with the rest of the Church in reality leads to a number of difficult choices. Those who want to can accuse CLC 2000 of inconsistency, sometimes going with *The Book of Common Prayer*, sometimes with Rome, sometimes with the British Isles, but the decision in each case was not arbitrary, but carefully weighed.

Aware of recent trends in worship

A second influence over the shape of the proposals, especially in terms of calendar, was more recent Church of England experiment after 1980. This came mainly through two books that have had widespread use. The first of these was *The Promise of His Glory*. Published in 1991, *The Promise of His Glory* provides calendar, lectionary, services and other texts for the period from All Saints' Day (1 November) until Candlemas (2 February). Prepared by the Liturgical Commission, it was debated in the General Synod and then commended by the House of Bishops for use. It advocated a unitive approach to the whole three month period, established a 'Kingdom' season from All Saints' Day until Advent, and made Candlemas a pivotal moment in the year, looking back to Christmas and forward to Easter. Widely used, it has already given people experience of calendar and lectionary that depart from the ASB.

The other publication was *Celebrating Common Prayer* (Mowbray, 1992). This was the work of a joint group of some members of the Liturgical Commission and members of religious communities, and in particular the Society of St Francis. What started as revision of the Franciscan Office Book, by the Society with the help of liturgical consultants, soon became a quest for a new form of Daily Prayer for the whole Church of England. It was and remains an unofficial publication, but, with archi-episcopal commendation and a distinguished list of compilers, it has widely established itself across the Church of England and beyond. In relation to CLC 2000, the significance is that *Celebrating Common Prayer* built upon the calendar proposals of *The Promise of His Glory*, accepted the Roman approach to some feasts and seasons, especially the relationship between Easter and Pentecost, and thus took those who used it one step further away from the ASB.

The Liturgical Commission believed that the direction in which these two books was taking the calendar was proving to be helpful. Thus another of its aims became to learn from those insights and to stay with them.

Recognizing saints days and festivals

A further aim – and this was another case where *Celebrating Common Prayer* had shown the way – was to look again at the way the Church of England celebrated the saints and heroes of the Church. The concern here was both to rethink how names were placed in the calendar and also how the celebration of the lives of those included could be made more memorable. This desire led to a new categorization of holy days, to the commemoration of many figures of our own century, to the redressing somewhat of the gender imbalance so that more women featured in the calendar, and to the provision of a collect for each festival and lesser festival, going well beyond previous official provision. (This is explored further in chapters 3 and 10).

The Alternative Service Book 1980 was widely seen as a very 'churchy' book, coming out of an era where the image of the Church that most appealed was 'the Body of Christ' and where distinctiveness from the world seemed more important than engagement with it. That, of course, is an over-simplification, but there is truth in it nevertheless. The ASB did not seem to want to make use of the opportunities presented by such days as Mothering Sunday, Harvest Thanksgiving or Remembrance Sunday. They received a mention, but they could not be celebrated without cutting across a quite different series of themes. The Commission wanted CLC 2000 to draw these popular 'folk' festivals into the liturgical cycle and to go 'with the grain', so to speak. This is reflected in, for instance, the collect and lectionary provision for both Mothering Sunday and Remembrance Sunday.

There was also a desire, first developed in *The Promise of His Glory*, to reclaim festivals that have become over-secularized, and to build on their popularity a new emphasis on Christian belief. Thus All Saintstide needs a higher profile, both to build on the secular celebration of Hallowe'en and also to correct it by sound Christian teaching and worship that rejoices in our communion with the saints.

Desire for commonality and memorability

The final principle at work in CLC 2000 is the one that was described earlier as a pressure to revise the 1980 provision. The Commission wanted a calendar, a lectionary and collect provision that would unite the Church and allow people moving from place to place to find themselves sharing everywhere in a common tradition. This meant that a new calendar needed to be compatible, as far as possible, with *The Book of Common Prayer*. It meant that there should be a fine lectionary, sufficiently well designed on good principles that very large numbers of people would choose to use it, to the extent that it would become a genuinely common lectionary. It meant having collects that were more concerned with commonality and memorability than with themes.

The aim is a fine one, though it has to be said that it was beyond the Commission's ability to put in place a further pillar of commonality, a single contemporary translation of Scripture for liturgical use. If the Church of England were to agree on such a version (CLC 2000 uses *The New Revised Standard Version* for its biblical references), it would mean a great step forward for the commonality of worship, and people would hear the Scriptures over and over again in the same words and begin to commit them, as former generations did, to memory. Whether the Church of England will find the will to do this remains to be seen.

CHRISTIAN YEAR: CHRISTIAN JOURNEY

This introductory chapter has told something of the background to CLC 2000. Most of the book (chapters 4 to 11) takes the reader through the Christian year, season by season and festival by festival, mainly with calendar questions in mind, but with some reference to lectionary and collect. Before that, in chapter 2, will come a full explanation of the lectionary, and in chapter 3 some background on collects. This first chapter ends with some words about the Christian year. They provide an introduction to the chapters that unfold the seasons one by one.

The Christian year operates at a number of levels. It is a marvellous teacher, putting people in remembrance through the seasons of the great stories of our redemption or, for some, proclaiming them for the first time. It is also a cycle of thanksgiving, for a Christian cannot hear these stories rehearsed year by year without being drawn into deep thanksgiving to God for the mysteries they unfold. The Christian year is also a means of entry into a lifestyle. Baptism commits the Christian to the way of Christ and, walking with Christ through the Christian year (supremely, of course, in Holy Week, but at other times also) the Christian is gradually drawn into that way, conformed to that pattern. Beyond that even, the Christian year, through its variety of moods and emphases and in its contrasts, enables us to make connections between our own life-cycle, with its ups and downs, joys and sorrows, and that of the Lord and his

Church, and within that connection there is potential for human growth and spiritual fruitfulness.

It is difficult to explain the cycle of the seasons in a way that goes beyond a straight description of what they recall and helps us to express how they affect Christian discipleship. But it has been very well put by Christopher Cocksworth and Alan Wilkinson in *An Anglican Companion* (SPCK/Church House Publishing, 1996):

The Christian year is like a journey – a journey we make as we walk the way of Christ. The *Sundays* of the year are milestones or markers along the way and the *festivals* stand out as peaks of the hills to which we are heading. The *seasons* define the sort of terrain which lies ahead. They form two groups. The first leads us through the coming of Christ. During *Advent* we climb towards the *Christmas* celebrations of Christ's presence among us, always with an eye searching for the distant horizon of Christ's coming at the end of time. From Christmas we travel through *Epiphany* as we see Christ revealed before us and then find this stage of the journey coming to an end on the *Day of the Presentation* as we discover that the Christ child, the light of the nations, is destined to suffer for all people.

The second group of seasons brings us through the saving events of Jesus' dying, rising, ascending and giving of the Spirit. A bridge between the two is provided by some Sundays which prepare us for the season of *Lent*. From *Ash Wednesday* it is clear that the path is pointing towards the passion of Christ. Towards the end of Lent each step is in the shadow of the cross and on Good Friday we stand at its foot.

Then comes the joy of *Easter* as the sun breaks through and we walk in the light of God's victory.

Still on the mountain top, the cloud of God's presence gathers Jesus from our sight at *Ascension*, but from the same cloud of glory comes the wind and fire of the Spirit refreshing his followers with the power of his presence at *Pentecost*.

The journey over the next few months may not have the same dramatic features of the last few weeks but *Trinity Sunday* calls us to keep travelling the road as bearers of the Spirit and as members of Christ for praise of the Father. As the autumn arrives, the journey moves both to its conclusion and to its new beginning. Advent once again beckons but before we arrive we celebrate, on *All Saints' Day*, those who have walked before us on the way of Christ and then we rejoice in *Christ the King* as we glimpse the kingdom for which we are called to work and pray.

2

Lectionary

THE REVISED COMMON LECTIONARY

No lectionary can be perfect, but there is much evidence that *The Revised Common Lectionary* is very good and that the Church of England has done a wise thing in giving approval to it as the heart of its calendar provisions for the year 2000.

The key dates in any brief history of *The Revised Common Lectionary* are 1969, 1983 and 1992. In 1969, as one of the fruits of the Second Vatican Council, the Roman Catholic Church adopted a quite new lectionary for Mass. This is the lectionary that forms the basis of what the Church of England has now adopted. In 1983 that Roman lectionary was published in an amended form as an ecumenical lectionary, given the name the 'Common Lectionary', and adopted by a number of Anglican provinces, including those in the United States and Canada. In 1992 the ecumenical Consultation on Common Texts published a revision of the Common Lectionary (a fairly minimal revision, except in one respect) and it is this lectionary, *The Revised Common Lectionary*, that is now being adopted by many churches. (In Britain it is published by the Canterbury Press.)

FAREWELL TO THE ASB LECTIONARY

For Anglicans in England, the appeal of *The Revised Common Lectionary* lies not only in its own merits but in the fact that the lectionary in *The Alternative Service Book* would seem to have had its day. Originally a production of the British ecumenical Joint Liturgical Group, it had been in use in the Church of England before 1980 and was then incorporated into the ASB. Four difficulties with its continued use have emerged:

1. There is a loss of ecumenical status. In 1980 it could be claimed for it that it was (a) the lectionary in widest use among non-Roman churches in Britain and (b) used in a number of Anglican provinces abroad. That was, of course, a strictly limited ecumenical appeal, not least because few of the Reformed Churches feel the same obligation to the lectionary that most Anglicans have (and which the canons enjoin), but there was appeal in it nonetheless. By 2000 there will probably be no other churches in Britain using it. One by one other churches and provinces are abandoning it.

2. A two-year cycle (especially one thematically determined) simply does not read sufficient Scripture. Of course that argument could be used against a three year lectionary or even a five year lectionary, and there is the need to create a balance between a wide selection to ensure the Bible is heard and a narrower selection to allow passages to be heard repeatedly and thus to establish themselves deeply. But a two year lectionary omits too much.

3. The ASB lectionary produced a lectionary-driven calendar, whereas the lectionary ought rather to be the servant of the Christian year. The ASB lectionary proceeded on a shape to the year that emphasized the First Person of the Trinity in the weeks before Christmas, the Second Person from Christmas till the Ascension, and the Third Person from Pentecost

through the summer. That is not a truly trinitarian approach, for God's operation is simply not like that, and God as Trinity is involved in every aspect of salvation history. But it has led to a lot of confusion, not least to the neutral 'green' period after Pentecost being regarded as an extended season of the Holy Spirit – 'of' Pentecost, rather than 'after' Pentecost.

4. The chief difficulty has been that the ASB themes have seemed increasingly inappropriate. It is not just that so many of them have 'worn thin'. It is, more fundamentally, that the predetermined theme approach is an improper way to use Scripture. It has produced a generation of Anglican preachers whose concern is more to identify the theme (and hope the readings bear it out) than to search the Scripture to see what it is saying. Of course it is not that Scripture does not have its themes or that it is wrong to find them. But it is the imposing of a pre-determined theme (and a unity between passages), rather than a prayerful searching of the particular texts or lections for their message on that day for that community, that is improper.

So much for the past. What of the future? Would the four-year lectionary, recently produced by the Joint Liturgical Group that pioneered the two-year lectionary, provide an answer? It works on a basis of one year for each Gospel. It was, no doubt, an interesting exercise for the Joint Liturgical Group to devise it, but it seems little short of perverse for a British ecumenical group to produce a lectionary obviously drawing on the insights of the Common Lectionary but refusing to go with it in fundamentals. The truth is that a 'year of John' is a difficult diet, John's Gospel being better spread through every year than all served up in one year, and this, as we shall see, is how *The Revised Common Lectionary* handles it. The Methodist Church, in a strangely immediate reaction, adopted this four-year lectionary, presumably expecting others to follow. None have done so and the Methodist Conference has now voted to go with *The Revised Common Lectionary*.

LECTIONARY PRINCIPLES

Eight lectionary principles seem to be at work in *The Revised Common Lectionary*:

1. It is a three-year cycle, each year being based on one of the synoptic Gospels. That Gospel provides the Gospel Reading whenever possible. This is not followed slavishly. There is not, for instance, a determination to find a Gospel Reading from Mark for Christmas Day. But, in general, one stays with one evangelist through a year, beginning to understand the distinctiveness of his style, his intention and his theology.
2. The Fourth Gospel is used in all three years, but especially in the second year, the 'year of Mark'. Because Mark is a considerably briefer Gospel than Matthew or Luke, there is space to read a good deal of John, though it occurs to some extent in the other two years as well. John is used only a little less than Luke, and much more than Mark, over the three years, so the fact that it does not have its own year does not imply any neglect of it.
3. The approach to the reading of the synoptic Gospels is in two parts. In the seasonal parts of the year, the readings are chosen from that Gospel to suit the feast or the season. Thus, in Advent, we have both

apocalyptic and John the Baptist, and there is no attempt to draw passages out of the Gospels in the order they occur there. But, in the non-seasonal part of the year, mainly the weeks after Trinity, the remaining passages – the ones not chosen for the seasons – are read in the order they occur in the Gospel semi-continuously.

4. The New Testament Reading (i.e. the Second Reading, what we have tended to call the 'Epistle', even when it is from Acts or Revelation) proceeds independently of the Gospel. New Testament letters are set at points in the year that marry well with the liturgical cycle, so there is a seasonal element to them, but there is no pre-determined connection between epistle and Gospel. New Testament letters are read semi-continuously in much the same way as the Gospels.

5. The Old Testament choices are approached rather differently. During the seasons, the Old Testament Reading links with the Gospel Reading, preparing for it, sometimes prefiguring it. The approach is seasonal, with even a hint of theme. But during non-seasonal, 'ordinary', time, there are two Old Testament tracks. One continues the approach whereby the Old Testament Reading anticipates the Gospel and relates fairly directly to it. The other track allows the Old Testament to speak for itself. Here Old Testament books are read semi-continuously, independently of New Testament Reading and Gospel, with no pre-determined link or theme.

6. The approach to psalmody is to provide one psalm for each set of readings. In almost every case it relates closely to the Old Testament Reading. Therefore, where there are two tracks for that reading, there are also two tracks for the psalm.

7. There is provision for readings from the Acts of the Apostles as the *First* reading in Eastertide: the Old Testament is not provided for on those eight Sundays, though there is rich Old Testament provision for a series of readings at the Easter Vigil. Acts followed by an Epistle is at first a surprise. It works remarkably well and becomes another way of marking out the Easter season as distinctive from the rest of the Christian year.

8. There are principles at work in relation to length of readings in *The Revised Common Lectionary*. They turn out to be, on average, just a little shorter than the ASB provision, but not markedly so. Just occasionally the lectionary allows a very long reading, particularly on three Sundays in Lent in Year A where long Johannine narratives – the woman at the well, the man born blind, the raising of Lazarus – are read in full. Were it to happen very often, it would be a problem. Coming as rarely as they do, they are three rather special Sundays and the stories all the more compelling for being told in their entirety.

DIFFERENCES FROM THE ROMAN MASS LECTIONARY

There are a number of points where *The Revised Common Lectionary* has chosen a different passage from the Roman Mass Lectionary, more often in the choice of the Old Testament Reading than any other. But, in terms of principles, *The Revised Common Lectionary* differs from the Roman Mass Lectionary only in three ways.

The first is that the Roman lectionary does not have the alternative Old Testament track in ordinary time that allows the First Reading to run quite independently of the Gospel. Secondly *The Revised Common Lectionary* always provides a canonical alternative to a reading from the Apocrypha in a way that the Roman lectionary does not. Thirdly, *The Revised Common Lectionary* is less keen to 'fillet' texts, that is, to omit verses here and there to produce a briefer passage with irrelevancies removed or even, sometimes, hard sayings suppressed. *The Revised Common Lectionary*, like all lectionaries, is not entirely free of filleting, but it does it less than Roman readings.

THE CHURCH OF ENGLAND AND
THE REVISED COMMON LECTIONARY

Faced with the existence of *The Revised Common Lectionary* at the moment when it came to revise its calendar and lectionary, the Church of England, through its Liturgical Commission, and later through its General Synod acting on the Commission's advice, had to enquire whether there were good reasons for not adopting it. That is the way the question was posed. For clearly there would need to have been compelling reasons for the Church of England to refuse to go with such a large majority of churches.

The Commission asked first: Is this lectionary reconcilable with our calendar? For, as we have already discussed, lectionary has to emerge from calendar, not the other way round. The calendar of the ASB followed in general the provision for the Christian year of most Western churches, though it was, at a few points, somewhat eccentric, particularly in its extended Advent, beginning on the Ninth Sunday before Christmas. In the latest revision, the Commission has encouraged the Church of England to be all the more in step, sometimes more in step with the modern Roman calendar and sometimes more in step with *The Book of Common Prayer*. *The Revised Common Lectionary* was compatible with the shape of the Christian year that the

Commission wished to commend. Only on a very few Sundays did the Commission find it necessary to recommend some deviation from *The Revised Common Lectionary* provision to satisfy calendrical requirements.

A second basic question that had to be addressed was this: Does *The Revised Common Lectionary* represent a sound approach to the reading of Scripture? The answer was emphatically 'Yes'. The Commission believed that it made for an approach to Scripture compatible with modern biblical scholarship, an approach that allowed the words of Scripture to speak for themselves and allowed the hearer to enter into the minds of the individual biblical writers in a way that a thematic approach, jumping from book to book, could never do.

Of course there were areas where *The Revised Common Lectionary* seemed to raise some problems. I mention six of them and how the Commission and later the Revision Committee addressed them.

The first related to creation and in particular to the first two chapters of Genesis. Here the lectionary was found to be weak. Its expectation was that Genesis 1 would always be read at the Easter Vigil, but the day is still far off when the presence of most Anglicans at that service can be guaranteed. Otherwise Genesis 1 is read in full only once every three years and that on Trinity Sunday. The account of creation in Genesis 2 is, extraordinarily, not set at all. But, more broadly, the lectionary shows no bias towards creation theology and, though it is probably wise for lectionaries to resist the temptation to be creatures of theological fashion, it would be odd for the Church of England, which in its Ninth Sunday before Christmas had, in effect, a 'Creation Sunday' to lose that altogether. The Commission's solution was to abandon *The Revised Common Lectionary* on the Second Sunday before Lent and to provide for that day readings that reflect the creation theme (and use the Genesis material). The choice of Sunday is partly in relation to the lectionary's own designation of the following Sunday (Next before Lent) as, in effect, 'Transfiguration Sunday', and also a desire to return to the period of the year when creation used to feature in the readings for Septuagesima. Celebration of creation leads now, via transfiguration, to celebration of redemption in the weeks of Lent and Passiontide.

A second strange omission from *The Revised Common Lectionary* is a good deal of the Book of Revelation. Lectionaries have always been understandably selective about Revelation, but none so selective as this one. Only three passages in the book feature before Revelation 21. The solution here has been to use Revelation widely in Second and Third Service lectionaries (more of these below), but also to add three Revelation readings in one year during the Epiphany season, so that there is a period when the book is read over a series of weeks.

The Revision Committee identified another strange omission: John's account of the woman caught in adultery. The story has now been made an alternative Gospel Reading on Ash Wednesday. Of course there remain other surprising omissions. Among them is the story of Cain and Abel, but, like most of *The Revised Common Lectionary* omissions, the Commission has brought these in to its Second and Third Service lectionaries.

Some anxiety was expressed about the lack of Old Testament provision in Eastertide. Not everyone shares this anxiety, but it seems unnecessarily restrictive not to allow Old Testament passages through those seven weeks, and quite inconvenient not to have some if this lectionary is being used at Morning or Evening Prayer where an Old Testament reading is ordered. The solution here, in order not to tinker too much with the lectionary, has been to reorder the Old Testament readings for the Easter Vigil for use on the Sundays of Eastertide as an alternative to the Acts of the Apostles.

The fifth problem related to the Sundays of the summer. The Commission was keen to retain (or for ASB users to return to) 'Sundays after Trinity' as the Sunday title. It was also anxious to attach familiar collects to these Sunday names, many of them the Prayer Book collects traditionally connected with particular named Sundays. *The Revised Common Lectionary*, however, calculates what readings should be used through the summer months not by Sunday after Trinity, but by Sunday between two calendar dates. (Not 'Third Sunday after Trinity', but what it calls 'Proper between June 19 and June 25 inclusive', for instance.) It was clear that collects could be attached to Sunday names or to sets of readings, but not to both. Sunday names and Sunday readings had to follow independent courses. Commission and Revision Committee both regretted this, but accepted it, and preferred the first option – collects attached to Sunday names. To have attached set readings to named Sundays would have destroyed the commonality of the lectionary and led to a foolishness where the Church of England followed the same lectionary as other churches, but on different days.

A final problem was the treatment of the Sundays of November. Here the Commission wanted the themes of the Kingdom, the Saints, the Life of Heaven and the Kingship of Christ strongly treated. It found *The Revised Common Lectionary* provision almost right for that set of emphases, but made a very few adjustments to strengthen this further.

The changes that the Church of England has made in *The Revised Common Lectionary* are minimal. Each change has been carefully weighed and each found to be worth making. But there has been a proper reluctance to make many changes. For a Common Lectionary can only be what it claims if churches are very sparing in the occasions that they deviate from it. By a discipline that has resisted too many alterations, the Church of England has kept faith with its ecumenical partners and is adopting a genuinely common lectionary.

Principal, second and third service lectionaries

Of course *The Revised Common Lectionary* is a one service lectionary. Its Roman antecedent is a Mass lectionary. *The Revised Common Lectionary* is not necessarily that. It is a 'principal service lectionary', eucharistic or otherwise, and for many churches that will be enough. For churches that need more, the Church of England has produced complementary lectionaries for second and third services on a Sunday. They use passages not in *The Revised Common Lectionary*, or not in it in that particular year. Like it, they are seasonal yet not thematic, and employ a semi-continuous approach to books especially in 'ordinary time'. Few readings in the ASB revision fail to find a place in one of the three lectionaries, and many passages, which did not feature in ASB, have found their way back in.

It is worth saying that, although the changes from *The Revised Common Lectionary* to the Church of England's Principal Service Lectionary are few, there are sufficient of them that anyone using *The Revised Common Lectionary* itself, or supplementary material based on it, will sometimes find themselves confused. In the end, it is not quite accurate to say that the Church of England is using *The Revised Common Lectionary*. It has authorized its own new lectionary, drawing very thoroughly in its principal service provision on *The Revised Common Lectionary*, and adding a good deal of further provision of its own.

In many ways it would have been easier to designate the principal service lectionary for use only at Holy Communion. But that would not have served well those congregations where the 'principal service' of the Sunday, in terms of attendance, has variable service forms – one week the Eucharist, another a Family Service, another Morning Prayer, for instance. It is undesirable for those who attend each week to be moving from one lectionary track to another. CLC 2000 makes its clear that they should not do so. It also intends consistency about the use of the Second and Third Service lectionaries. Note 8 on the Lectionary reads: 'Three sets of psalms and readings are provided for each Sunday'.

The First Sunday Lectionary (which is drawn from *The Revised Common Lectionary*) is intended for use at the principal service of the day (whether this service is the Holy Communion or some other authorized form). In most church communities, this is likely to be the mid-morning service, but the minister is free to decide which service time normally constitutes the principal service of the day.

The Second Sunday Lectionary is intended for a second main service. In many churches, this lectionary will be the appropriate provision for a Sunday afternoon or evening service. A Gospel reading is always provided so that this lectionary can, if necessary, be used at the Holy Communion.

The Third Sunday Lectionary, with shorter readings, is intended where a third set of psalms and readings is needed and is most appropriate for use at an office.

None of this provision is intended to prevent the use of the Epistle and Gospel from *The Book of Common Prayer* at a celebration of Holy Communion, where that seems appropriate.

EXERCISING OPTIONS

There are two areas where the minister has to make decisions that affect the balance of Scripture heard as well as its intelligibility to the hearers.

The first relates to which readings should be chosen when less than three are being used. Sometimes this will be because the service form requires only two, but sometimes because a pastoral decision has been taken to read less. Note 6 deals with this question thus:

> When there are only two readings at the principal service and that service is Holy Communion, the second reading is always the Gospel reading.
>
> In the choice of readings other than the Gospel reading, the Minister should always ensure that, in any year, a balance is maintained between readings from the Old Testament and New Testament and that, where a particular book is appointed to be read over several weeks, the choice ensures that this continuity of one book is not lost.
>
> When the principal service lectionary is used at a service other than Holy Communion, the Gospel reading need not always be chosen.

The balance that is being sought here means a questioning of the Anglican bias towards an 'Epistle' rather than an Old Testament Reading at the Eucharist. It is derived from the Prayer Book provision, but the Prayer Book compilers assumed the faithful would hear long Old Testament readings at Morning and Evening Prayer.

The ASB lectionary, with its asterisked reading, tried to establish that, where there were only two readings, the Old Testament was sometimes to be preferred. The new provision urges the same principle, but leaves the decision to the local minister.

The other question of this sort relates to the choice of Old Testament Reading on the Sundays after Trinity. The choice reflects two approaches to Scripture, one that begins with the Gospel and makes other provision in the light of it, another that wants the Old Testament to stand on its own. Note 11 describes the issue thus:

> On the Sundays after Trinity, the Principal Service Lectionary provides alternative Old Testament readings and psalms. Those in the right-hand column relate the Old Testament reading and the psalm to the Gospel reading. Those in the left-hand column allow the Old Testament reading and its complementary psalm to stand independently of the other readings. It is unhelpful to move from week to week from one column to other. One column should be followed for the whole sequence of Sundays after Trinity.

'It is unhelpful' is rubrical language for 'it is nonsensical'. It may be that a church will always stay with one 'column' because it believes it to be the sounder way of reading Scripture. But, if there is to be variety of approach, it needs to be from year to year, not week to week.

The Revised Common Lectionary makes little provision for saints' days. Most of what has been provided in CLC 2000 is therefore the work of the Liturgical Commission. In this area, it has allowed itself to be influenced by both Prayer Book and Roman Missal, as well as by other Anglican provision. It provides more than the ASB, including an optional 'First Evening Prayer' on the eve of a festival, and a richer collection from which to choose readings for lesser festivals. Among these it recommends particular readings for particular days where something is overwhelmingly appropriate.

NEW LECTIONARY: FRESH PREACHING

The question of preaching is mainly outside the subject matter of this book, but it is important to spell out that a new Sunday lectionary, operating on different principles, will provide real challenge (and opportunity) to the preacher. For a clergy and other preachers who have known nothing but the ASB and its themes, the withdrawal of pre-determined themes, so that the preacher must come with an open mind and heart to the particular texts or lections appointed and search there for a theme, may be threatening. It is never that there is no theme; themes emerge from every creative engagement with the Scriptures. But they do come from that engagement, not from some pre-determined list.

Sometimes a preacher will find a creative relationship among all three readings and will knit the passages together in preaching. But that will not always be the case. Sometimes the preacher will opt to preach about one of the passages set, and let the others speak for themselves, as they so often will.

Yet it will be helpful in planning preaching, in a church where several people are part of a preaching 'team', to look together at the points where new biblical books come 'on line'. If Ephesians, for instance, is being read for four weeks, it may be sensible to let it speak for itself in weeks two, three and four and get on with preaching about the Gospel, but in week one it will be important for the preacher to signal that for a few weeks Ephesians will be part of the Liturgy of the

Word and perhaps to say something of its authorship and its major themes.

The new lectionary offers a fresh stimulus to preaching, provided that preachers respond to the challenge, strive to engage with a new approach and steadfastly refuse to take the short cuts that will no doubt be provided by helpful authors who will soon detect some unofficial themes worth sharing in print.

3

The collects

CLC 2000 provides the Church of England with its richest provision yet of collects and adds another major provision of a second prayer for use after communion at the Eucharist. There is a collect and a 'post communion', as it is called, for every Sunday and for every Principal Holy Day, Festival and Lesser Festival, and also for the 'common' of saints and for a variety of special occasions. Much of *The Book of Common Prayer* material is retained (or reappears after an absence from ASB 1980) and other sources are drawn upon in this large collection, but there is also much new work, principally among the Lesser Festival collects and the post-communions.

The collect form is very familiar to Anglicans, and the weekly collect of the Prayer Book has become the model for many books full of collect-type prayers, though few have been able to stay with the constraints of the disciplined pithy style of many ancient collects that the Prayer Book translates in a memorable way. Even Thomas Cranmer, when he composed a fresh prayer, was tempted into more fulsome expression than most classic ancient collects, and today that remains a difficulty with collect writing – too often the writer wants to say too much.

Whereas the collect form is familiar, the use of the collect is far less understood. Recent revision has tried to regain the sense of the collect as a prayer that draws together a time of corporate silent praying (see below). But there has been within Anglicanism a long tradition that sees the collect in a different way, and the compilers of the collects in CLC 2000 were anxious to hold on to this Anglican approach. This is the approach that sees the collect as essentially a 'prayer for the week', a particular text identified with a particular Sunday and the weekdays that follow it. The fact that the Prayer Book went for a weekly collect, with little variation for saints' days and the like, meant that the repetition of the collect two or three times a day drew it into the memory, in a way that is not possible if there is a different collect at every service or if collects are controlled more by time of day or by season than by week.

Less frequent church attendance, the ASB's removal of some Prayer Book collects altogether and the relocation of others to different Sundays, and a culture not much interested in memory have all contributed to the partial collapse of this Anglican phenomenon of the weekly collect at least half known by heart by the faithful, but the Liturgical Commission's proposals try to resist any further collapse. For this reason they set themselves against the approach of some other provinces and of the new Roman Missal in having a different collect in each year of the three-year cycle, tying the collect more closely to that year's lections on that day.

Indeed the approach of CLC 2000 moves the Church of England away from any idea of the collect as a theme prayer. Its approach to collects is thoroughly seasonal, but does not go the extra step of making them thematic. The ASB, with its essentially thematic approach to readings, complemented these with thematic collects. Thus, for instance, on The Seventh Sunday before Christmas, when the readings at the Sunday Eucharist were about the patriarch Abraham, the collect for the week also focused on Abraham, even at services when the Abraham lections were not in use. With the abandonment of the thematic approach to lectionary, and with the decision to stay with the one collect across three years, CLC 2000 sets itself against thematic collects and makes it clear that, in the Eucharist, the collect is not the first element in the Liturgy of the Word, but the last element in the Preparation.

The Liturgical Commission's aim, revealed in Holy Communion Rites A & B Revised, is to restore the collect as the 'collecting' presidential prayer at the end of a time of corporate praying. In the Eucharist the classic form of this praying is an invitation by the president, 'Let us pray', followed by a time of silent prayer and then the collect to draw it all together. In this view it is not so much collecting up themes as collecting up individual praying and giving it a 'corporate seal'. In Morning and Evening Prayer, at least in the form they appear in *Celebrating Common Prayer* or the Roman Catholic Daily Prayer, the collect comes at the end of a period of thanksgiving and intercession, and fulfils much the same function. The difference essentially is that, in the Eucharist, the collect is the 'opening prayer', whereas, in the office, it is the 'concluding prayer'. Rites A & B Revised give far more encouragement to those who lead worship than did the ASB to introduce the collect with 'Let us pray', or a more extended bidding, to make the silent prayer more than a mere pause, and then to use the collect to 'draw together'.

That is, in the Commission's understanding, its principal function, though if the Sunday collect can also carry its established Anglican function of being also the 'prayer of the week', so much the better.

It follows that CLC 2000 makes provision for only one collect on any occasion (though there is another prayer for use after communion at the Eucharist). If the function of the collect is to draw together, a second collect, far from drawing together, introduces another strand of thinking at an unhelpful point in the development of the service. Where there is a subsidiary idea to find a place (perhaps the commemoration of a saint) it is better included in the Prayers of Intercession than in the collect form.

THE SUNDAY COLLECTS OF CLC 2000

The starting point for the collects of CLC 2000, in relation to Principal Holy Days, Sundays and Festivals, is the provision of collects in *The Book of Common Prayer*. Not all of them have been used as the collect of the day, but rather more than in the ASB and, although it is a subjective matter, the compiling group believed they had retained all the best and most loved Prayer Book collects, save for one or two that could not be rendered in a contemporary form without doing violence to them. The collection includes a number of Prayer Book collects not found in ASB 1980, among them the collects for Christmas Day, Epiphany and The Presentation. In the latter two cases the ASB had substituted, presumably because the task of rendering them in a satisfactory contemporary form had proved difficult, new prayers that were not theologically as rich. A comparison of the Prayer Book, ASB and CLC 2000 collects for Epiphany reveals the kind of policy that the new provision reflects:

BCP

O God, who by the leading of a star didst manifest thy only-begotten Son to the Gentiles: mercifully grant, that we, which know thee now by faith, may after this life have the fruition of thy glorious godhead; through . . .

ASB

Eternal God,
who by the shining of a star
led the wise men to the worship of your Son:
guide by his light the nations of the earth,
that the whole world may behold your glory;
    through . . .

CLC 2000

O God,
who by the leading of a star
manifested your only Son
    to the peoples of the earth:
mercifully grant that we,
who know you now by faith,
may at the last behold your glory face to face;
    through . . .

In most cases, collects drawn from the Prayer Book have been assigned to their Prayer Book date. ASB 1980 had moved them around in the interests of its thematic approach. CLC 2000 keeps them on their traditional date, except where there is good reason to do otherwise. The good reasons include the desire to move strongly penitential collects to Lent and to ensure a more paschal flavour to Eastertide. Thus, for instance, the Prayer Book's collect for The Third Sunday after Easter ('Almighty God, who shewest to them that be in error the light of thy truth, to the intent that they may return into the way of righteousness . . .'), which has little resonance of the resurrection, is moved in CLC 2000 to The Second Sunday in Lent, where its call 'to reject those things that are contrary to our profession' strikes the right note near the beginning of Lent. The Prayer Book collect for Easter Day (the ASB makes it an alternative to a new collect) is retained within Eastertide, but not on Easter Day itself, for it lacks the note of triumph and joy of the ASB alternative on this feast of feasts.

A decision was taken at an early stage to render all the Prayer Book collects into contemporary liturgical language. Although there is a greater willingness than in the recent past to mix traditional and contemporary liturgical language in one service, it was recognized that, in churches where the language of worship is almost exclusively contemporary, there was a need for the collects to conform to the norm. In rewriting Prayer Book collects in a contemporary form, the compilers tried hard to balance the sometimes conflicting claims of plain straightforward intelligibility on the one hand and the familiar resonances and rhythms of the Prayer Book on the other. Some will feel that some anachronisms have slipped through; others will feel that too much has been sacrificed. But each individual decision was made with care and the Revision Committee received very few amendments to the Commission's original work in this area.

There is, in any case, a note to allow those who wish to use the text of the Prayer Book collects as they stand. It reads:

> An asterisk against the word collect or post-communion indicates that this is a collect to be found in a traditional form in the *The Book of Common Prayer*, and that that traditional form may be used in place of the text provided here.

There are two Prayer Book collects where the Revision Committee was faced with compelling arguments to amend the Prayer Book wording in order to recover the original sense of the Latin lost in the Prayer Book rendering. In the provision for Trinity 4, where CLC 2000 uses the Prayer Book collect, the Prayer Book words

> . . . that, thou being our ruler and guide,
> we may so pass through things temporal,
> that we finally lose not the things eternal

have been amended in the interests of accuracy and richer theological meaning to read in CLC 2000:

> . . . that with you as our ruler and guide
> we may so pass through things temporal
> that we lose not our hold on things eternal.

Similarly, the Prayer Book's collect for Trinity 6 which reads

> . . . pour into our hearts such love toward thee,
> that we, loving thee above all things,
> may obtain thy promises,
> which exceed all that we can desire

has been amended in the collect for the same Sunday in CLC 2000 to read:

> . . . pour into our hearts such love towards you
> that we, loving you in all things
>   and above all things,
> may obtain your promises,
> which exceed all that we can desire.

The collects that were new to the Church of England in *The Alternative Service Book* also feature in the new provision. The only ones to be dropped are those tied to too narrow a theme, such as the Abraham and Moses collects before Christmas. But there have been a number of attempts to recast in order to achieve either greater clarity of meaning or greater felicity of expression.

Thus, for instance, ASB's collect for Pentecost 12, reads:

Almighty God,
who called your Church to witness
that you were in Christ reconciling men to yourself:
help us so to proclaim the good news of your love,
that all who hear it may be reconciled to you;
through him who died for us and rose again
and reigns with you and the Holy Spirit,
one God, now and for ever.

This becomes in the CLC 2000 collect for Trinity 13:

Almighty God,
who called your Church to bear witness
that you were in Christ
    reconciling the world to yourself:
help us to proclaim the good news of your love,
that all who hear it may be drawn to you;
through him who was lifted up on the cross,
and reigns with you in the unity of the Holy Spirit,
one God, now and for ever.

The change from 'witness' to 'bear witness' reads better, the change from 'reconciling all men' to 'reconciling the world' deals with the inclusive language issue in an acceptable way, the use of 'drawn to you' avoids an infelicitous repetition of 'reconciled', and the 'lifted up on the cross' stays with the 'drawn to you' image and makes the reference to the cross more explicit. Altogether the prayer is much improved. There are several similar examples.

In the Sunday provision, a number of collects are drawn from *The Promise of His Glory* (where most were from ancient sources, rather than new compositions), and in general this is not an area where the compilers have been ready to compose new material. It is a different story with the provision for saints' days.

THE COLLECTS FOR SAINTS' DAYS

In CLC 2000, where the Prayer Book provides a collect for a particular saint's day, that has usually been taken as the starting point, though occasionally a different collect in the ASB has been followed. But the Prayer Book provision is sparse and even the ASB provided few collects for lesser festivals. This therefore represents an area of considerable creativity by the Commission and the Revision Committee. Two earlier unofficial productions provided sources. One was *Celebrating Common Prayer*, which followed the ASB calendar (in general), but provided collects for its lesser festivals. The other was *The Cloud of Witnesses* (published for the Alcuin Club by Collins in 1982). George Timms' collects in *The Cloud of Witnesses* are often too narrow (ending up praying for the ordained ministry, rather than the whole Church) and defy 'inclusivization'. Nevertheless they were formative in creating a demand for an individual collect for each 'lesser festival'. CLC 2000 now provides this, drawing on both books. But the majority are new compositions or local material now given national recognition. The collect for Wulfstan of Worcester is based on one used at Worcester Cathedral, that for Julian of Norwich the one written for her shrine in Norwich, that for Cuthbert the one used in Durham, that for Etheldreda the one in Ely.

In creating new texts, the Commission also drew not only on the theological writings of those being commemorated, but even on their own prayers, sometimes stretching the collect form to its limits to achieve this. Obvious examples are Richard of Chichester (16 June), Lancelot Andrewes (25 September), Alfred the Great (26 October) or this for Alcuin of York (20 May):

God of Wisdom, Eternal Light,
who shone in the heart of your servant Alcuin,
revealing to him your power and pity:
scatter the darkness of our ignorance
that, with all our heart and mind and strength,
we may seek your face
and be brought with all your saints
to your holy presence; through . . .

which is based on Alcuin's own prayer:

Eternal Light, shine into our hearts;
eternal Goodness, deliver us from evil;
eternal Power, be our support,
eternal Wisdom, scatter the darkness of our
    ignorance;
eternal Pity, have mercy on us;
that with all our heart and mind and strength
    we may seek your face
and be brought by your infinite mercy
    to your holy presence;
through Jesus Christ our Lord.

There is also a provision of 'common' collects, for martyrs, teachers, pastors and other categories. Within the
final category of 'Any Saints' are collects for Christian
rulers, for those who worked with the poor and under-
privileged, for men and women of learning and for
those whose holiness was revealed in marriage and
family life. These help to balance provision for saints
that very often sees sanctity in narrow terms. These
common collects are available when a decision is taken
to make one of the 'commemorations' into a 'lesser
festival', thus creating a need to provide a collect for it.
They are also available for the kind of local festivals, in
a diocesan calendar, that CLC 2000 encourages, though
here it would be good if, within each diocese, work was

done on collects for those local saints and heroes the diocese wished to celebrate.

The collect provision ends with collects for a host of special occasions and needs – the guidance of the Holy Spirit, the peace of the world, the unity of the Church, for instance. In general these are the categories found in the Prayer Book of 1928 and in the ASB. But additionally there is provision for 'Social Justice and Responsibility', for 'The Sovereign', and for 'Ministry', which includes Ember Days, but broadens the field with other collects, including one for the beginning of a new ministry.

POST COMMUNIONS

CLC 2000 provides a prayer after communion for each occasion. It is intended to be a presidential variable text, usually preceding an almost invariable congregational one, and it brings a seasonal element to the final part of the rite. *The Alternative Service Book* allows for a variable post communion in Rite A, but provides no texts. Rites A and B Revised speak of the post communion prayer. The Roman Missal provides such a prayer and some Anglican provinces have also done so in recent revisions, notably the Canadian *Book of Alternative Services*. In England *The Promise of His Glory, Patterns for Worship* (Church House Publishing, 1989, 1995) and *Enriching the Christian Year* (SPCK, 1992) have all paved the way.

The Commission's decision was that not all these prayers need be specifically eucharistic in reference. This was for two reasons. Firstly it was because an examination of other sets of post communions revealed that there are a limited number of ways in which season or saint's day can be linked with thanksgiving for communion. The result is a certain sameness to the prayers. Secondly it was because a decision not to make every prayer eucharistic broadened the field to allow many fine collects that would otherwise be lost to have a place in this provision.

CLC 2000's post communion prayers therefore include collects from the Prayer Book, from ASB 1980 and other sources. They tend to be the short tightly constructed collects and the ones that have an element of 'sending out' to them. However, the majority come from other sources, drawing on the books already mentioned, and also including a great deal of new writing. In particular, nearly all the saints' day post communions have been written for CLC 2000, and they represent a considerable body of new prayer material from the Commission.

A word needs to be said about the Prayer Book provision for the use throughout Advent of the collect of Advent 1 and throughout Lent of the Ash Wednesday collect after the collect of the day. The ASB made no such provision, but the use has continued in many places. The new proposals, because they envisage only one collect, propose another solution. They propose the use of the Advent 1 collect as the post communion prayer from Advent 2 to Christmas Eve and of the Ash Wednesday collect as the post communion prayer from Lent 2 until the day before Lent 5 as alternatives to the variable post communions already provided. They can therefore be used to give cohesion to the season and to bring back the seasonal emphasis at the end without introducing a superfluous collect earlier.

Ending the collect and the post-communion

In the past Church of England collects have sometimes been provided with a 'short ending' – 'through Jesus

Christ our Lord' – and sometimes with a longer ending
– 'through Jesus Christ your Son our Lord, who is alive
and reigns with you, in the unity of the Holy Spirit, one
God, now and for ever'. The exact wording of the endings has varied according to the sense of the collect and
there have been a variety of conventions about exactly
how the longer ending is worded. Some leaders of worship have always added the longer ending to the collect
of the day, and the ASB specifically makes allowance
for that. The proposals that the Commission presented
to the synod took a similar line. The text contained a
mixture of long and short endings for the collect, with
a note to indicate that the longer version might always
be used, and with specific encouragement to use this
longer form at the Eucharist.

It was the Revision Committee that decided on a
different approach. Keen to see the longer ending as
the norm, thus ending the collect with a trinitarian
'formula', the Committee returned the proposals to the
Synod with the long ending printed in every case. This
was accepted, but the House of Bishops wisely added
before Final Approval a note to allow the short ending
where the minister so decides and where the collect
makes sense with a simple 'through Jesus Christ our
Lord'.

The Revision Committee also brought clarity to the
question of ending the post communion prayer. Here
tradition does not go for a trinitarian ending, but for a
simple christological one. Whereas the Commission's
original set of post-communions was not entirely con-
sistent in this respect, the post communions now end
in a uniform set of ways, most with 'Christ our Lord',
others, where the sense requires, 'who is alive and
reigns, now and for ever'.

4

Advent to Candlemas

THE SEASON OF ADVENT

CLC 2000 is quite clear that The First Sunday of Advent
is the first Sunday of the Christian year. At the other end
of the year there may be 'Sundays before Advent', but
there is no doubt that Advent marks the beginning.
Gone is the ASB's Nine Sundays before Christmas with
its beginning to the liturgical cycle in late October.

In pastoral terms Advent tends to be a season that
moves bit by bit towards Christmas. The stages at which
different elements that properly belong to Christmas
find their way in during Advent depend on pastoral
decisions taken in the light of the need of the local community. A school carol service, for instance, may have
to be earlier in Advent than the parish priest would like
simply because the school's end of term so dictates. To
some extent parishes learn to live in two worlds – keeping fairly strictly to Advent in the main Sunday liturgy,
but letting Christmas in for special events preparing the
wider community for the Christmas festival.

In terms of calendar and lectionary, Advent is not so
much a season of gradual development, though there is
an element of that, but of a season in two parts with a
shift, at least in terms of readings, on 17 December. In
the period from Advent 1 until 16 December, collects
and readings give emphasis to Advent as a period of
preparation for the Second Coming, the return of Christ
as judge at the end of the world. The Advent hymns are,

46

of course, full of this theme and the 'Come, Lord, come' that people sing enthusiastically is much more about that second coming than about the birth at Bethlehem.

17 December is the day called *O Sapientia*. There are a series of fine antiphons that look forward to the coming of Christ, drawing on Old Testament imagery and a variety of pictures of the coming Messiah. Traditionally they were sung before and after *Magnificat* at Evening Prayer. They are known as the 'Great Advent Antiphons' or sometimes simply as the 'Great O's'. They form the basis of the Advent hymn, 'O come, O come, Emmanuel', and indeed the last of the antiphons is *O Emmanuel*. The texts can be found in a number of liturgical sources (with music, for instance, in *The New English Hymnal*) and are treated in several different ways in *The Promise of His Glory*. For their original use at Evening Prayer, though it may still be found, has more often given way to a more creative use in Advent Carol Services and other special liturgies or in prayers during the Advent season. CLC 2000 is content to say 'From 17 December (*O Sapientia*) begin the eight days of prayer before Christmas Day'. It is a kind of 'count down' to Christmas, and in readings and prayers the emphasis on the second coming gives way to preparation to celebrate again the first coming at Bethlehem.

There is a little confusion of which to be wary. The antiphons attracted an additional rogue antiphon in medieval times, out of character with the others because it was addressed not to the Coming Lord, but to his mother. *O Virgo Virginum* appeared on 23 December, and forced the others back a day, which is why *The Book of Common Prayer* gives 16, not 17, December as *O Sapientia*.

Because the liturgical cycle is always a subtle instrument of the Gospel, it is almost too simple to say that

Advent divides into two parts. There are other currents that cut across that simplicity. One is John the Baptist. At one level, he belongs with second coming talk, for his message is one of repentance and of judgement, and as a man in the wilderness he does not belong with the infancy narratives at all. Nevertheless the stories of his own conception and birth are inseparably linked with the stories of the Lord's conception and birth, as Luke tells it, and the story of the Visitation brings the two mothers-to-be together. The figure of John must be allowed to make its impact. The readings for Advent 2 begin to focus on him and then, on Advent 3, there is more of John, and the collect alludes to him. (This is different from the Prayer Book sequence where John occupies Advent 3 and Advent 4).

The introduction of John the Baptist would make the observance of Bible Sunday on Advent 2 even more difficult than in the past. It established itself on Advent 2 because of the Prayer Book collect for that day ('Blessed Lord, who hast caused all holy Scriptures to be written for our learning . . .'), but it has always been a pity that Advent has no sooner started than we are diverted into a theme which, however important, draws attention away from the major thrust of Advent. CLC 2000 therefore moves Bible Sunday, complete with the familiar collect and sets of lections to the last Sunday after Trinity at the end of October (see chapter 8).

The Promise of His Glory encouraged an approach to Advent where not too many saints' days are allowed to deflect from the integrity of the season. CLC 2000 does not overload the calendar with saints in December and, in any case, not every lesser festival listed need be celebrated as such, and some days may be better as commemorations (see chapter 10). Three festivals, however, do not so much cut across the season as add to the build-up towards Christmas. The first is 6 December, the Feast of St Nicholas, with its identification with Santa Claus. The second, 8 December, The Conception of the Blessed Virgin Mary, a Prayer Book observance that ASB omitted, has something of the mood of a day of 'Our Lady in Advent', and the use of the story of the Fall (Genesis 3.8–15) in contrast to the Annunciation story (Luke 1.26–38) as the Gospel provokes a helpful series of reflections. 13 December is the Feast of St Lucy. The fact that Lucy was a martyr at Syracuse early in the fourth century is perhaps less important than that on one of the shortest darkest days of winter, whilst the Church is preparing to celebrate the coming into the darkness of Christ the Light, there occurs the festival of a saint whose name means 'light'. Furthermore there are of course links between the observance of Lucy's festival in Scandinavia and the Advent ring or wreath, with its lights, that now adorn our churches in Advent.

Nicholas, the Conception and Lucy are all examples of days that are not crucial to the Christian cycle, can be ignored and in some places have to be, but which can be used creatively in preparing people for Christmas if leaders of worship and directors of Advent carol services will let their imaginations engage with the possibilities.

One other saint's day needs to be mentioned. 21 December is, in the Prayer Book and through most of Christian history, the feast of St Thomas the Apostle. Modern Roman observance moved it to 3 July. It is almost too close on 21 December to Christmas to have much chance of celebration, and the story of Thomas is such an important one that it ought not to be lost. ASB 1980 followed Rome, as have most Anglican provinces, in opting for 3 July. CLC 2000 does the same, but by note permits its celebration on its traditional date in December.

The Fourth Sunday of Advent, always falling within the 'count down' period marked by the Advent antiphons, has, as its Gospel in the three years, the annunciation to Joseph, the annunciation to Mary and the visit of Mary to Elizabeth. These give shape to this day, as do the collect and post-communion, bringing the Church to the tiptoe of expectation with Christmas very near, without anticipating the Christmas story itself. There is also provision for Christmas Eve, but this is not used when Advent 4 falls on a Sunday.

THE TWELVE DAYS OF CHRISTMAS

Christmas Day inaugurates a time of celebration that runs for forty days until Candlemas, but it begins with the twelve days of Christmas that are still part of secular perception of the Christian year. The CLC 2000 calendar notes 'the days after Christmas Day until the Epiphany traditionally form a unity of days of special thanksgiving'. In other words, where there remains some thought of Christmas having an 'octave', a week of celebration after it, this should be forgotten. It is the whole twelve days to Epiphany that are marked out as a period of particular joy and festivity.

Christmas is the first of nine 'Principal Feasts' of the Christian year listed in CLC 2000. (The others are The Epiphany, The Presentation, The Annunciation, Easter Day, Ascension Day, Pentecost, Trinity Sunday and All Saints' Day.) In the case of Christmas, the requirements of canon law probably need little enforcement. Nevertheless CLC 2000 notes that on Principal Feasts 'the Holy Communion is celebrated in every cathedral and parish church, and this celebration, required by Canon B 14, may only be dispensed with in accordance with the provision of Canon B14A'.

The note goes on to say that Christmas and Easter, unlike the other principal feasts, do not have a 'First Evening Prayer' on the day before. The feast begins with the midnight Eucharist. Evening Prayer on Christmas Eve retains the sense of waiting and anticipation and has its own Christmas Eve collect. The change comes with the Eucharist, whether this begins at midnight or somewhat earlier.

The principal service lectionary gives three sets of three readings and psalm. Most straightforwardly these are for use at the Eucharist of midnight, the dawn and the morning, and where a church has three celebrations this may be the way to use them. But many churches will not have three Eucharists and in some others the order of the three sets will need reversing. Following ancient tradition the Gospel given for the middle of the night is Luke 2.1–14 and the Gospel for the last of the three, in the middle of the morning, John 1.1–14. But there are many communities where John 1.1–14 seems to work better in the middle of the night, at a solemn service, with an adult congregation, and Luke 2.1–14 better in the morning when children are present. CLC 2000 recognizes the need for flexibility and allows the minister to order the lectionary material in the way that seems most helpful, but it does require the use of Set III (Isaiah 52.7–10, Psalm 98, Hebrews 1.1–4 [5–12] and John 1.1–14) at some point during the celebration.

Unlike the ASB, CLC 2000 does not require the transfer of St Stephen, St John or the Holy Innocents to 29 December if one of them falls on a Sunday. Permission to transfer them remains, but they may be kept on a Sunday. If they have been placed in the calendar immediately after Christmas Day, it is because they have something important to add to the Christmas festival. To move them to a weekday in the very years when they have the chance to make their impact seems foolish. It is difficult to imagine 'the feast of Stephen' on anything but 26 December. So any of these three days may take precedence over the celebration of 'The First Sunday of Christmas', as may The Naming and Circumcision of Jesus when 1 January falls, like Christmas Day, on a Sunday.

It is common sense to do so, but Lectionary Note 6 requires the reading of Acts 7.51–60 on St Stephen's Day. It would be an odd decision to use the Old Testament reading and the Gospel on that day and omit the New Testament reading with its account of the stoning of Stephen, but stranger things have happened.

Two small points of nomenclature may be noted. The first is that the Sundays are called 'Sundays *of* Christmas', not 'after Christmas'. Christmas is a season, not a single day, and this is emphasized by speaking of the Sundays thus. The second is that CLC 2000 calls 1 January 'The Naming and Circumcision of Jesus'. The ASB had lost 'The Circumcision' and replaced it with 'The Naming'. The new calendar recognizes that there is some theological significance in the circumcision story and that it should not be lost in the title of the day. Provision for the secular New Year's Day is likely to follow when the Commission publishes its *Book of Times and Seasons* (a provisional working title), that will fill out the liturgical provision for the year. Meanwhile the post-communion prayer for The Naming has more than a hint of it:

> . . . grant that we who have shared
> in this sacrament of our salvation
> may live out our years in the power
> of the name above all other names,
> Jesus Christ our Lord.

Those who believe that St Stephen, St John and the

Holy Innocents are enough saints for the twelve days of Christmas can note that St Thomas Becket, a lesser festival on 29 December, may be transferred to the traditional date of his 'translation', 7 July.

EPIPHANY

The Promise of His Glory made much of the fact that Epiphany is more than 'the kings', but a season that celebrates the revelation of Christ's glory in a variety of ways, but principally through three great Bible stories – the Coming of the Magi, the Baptism of the Lord and the First Miracle at Cana, when water was turned into wine. To do justice to those three stories and to explore their theological significance, let alone to find room for other supporting lections and themes, CLC 2000 opts firmly for a season 'of Epiphany', rather than simply 'after Epiphany', and for an ending to it as late as 2 February even in a year when Lent begins early.

The ASB was ambivalent about Epiphany. It ordered white as the liturgical colour until and including The First Sunday after Epiphany, with its theme of the Lord's baptism, and then returned to green, as if the incarnation season was over. Yet it continued to order an Epiphany preface at the Eucharist and many of the collects and lections still had an Epiphany flavour. There is no such ambivalence about CLC 2000. The celebration of the incarnation season continues until Candlemas, Sundays are '*of* Epiphany', the first of them is (almost always) called 'The Baptism of Christ', Epiphany collects and lections continue through four Sundays of Epiphany, the Cana Miracle (John 2.1–11) is read at a principal service every year, and white remains the liturgical colour throughout the season. So much for official provision; obviously that needs to be reflected in choices of hymns and other music, in a decision on how long to retain the Christmas crib in church and in other local decisions that give this extended forty-day Christmas–Epiphany period its character.

Except when Easter is very late, there are always some Sundays to be 'lost' between Epiphany and Lent. The Prayer Book and the ASB lose them from Epiphany. Thus, with an early Easter, The Prayer Book's 'Septuagesima' or the ASB's 'Ninth Sunday before Lent' fall in January, long before Candlemas, and Epiphany has only a couple of Sundays. This cannot happen with the new calendar. All Sundays until 2 February are 'of Epiphany'. Where Sundays have to be 'lost', they are the Sundays 'before Lent' (see chapter 5).

The Feast of the Epiphany itself is one of those nine days designated as a 'Principal Feast', when Holy Communion must be celebrated and nothing must take precedence over the celebration. As a principal feast, it has a first Evening Prayer, with appropriate readings and the Epiphany collect. There was considerable discussion in the Commission and the Revision Committee on whether there should be permission always to transfer the Epiphany to a Sunday. The view that won the day was that, if possible, the Epiphany should be kept on its 'proper' day at the end of the twelve days of Christmas. There was a sense in which the Twelve Days of Christmas would be undermined by its observance on a Sunday before 6 January. Equally its transfer to the Sunday after 6 January undermined the celebration of the Baptism of Christ on that Sunday. In the end a note that has a certain reluctance to it declares: 'In any year when there is a Second Sunday of Christmas, the Epiphany (6 January) may, for pastoral reasons, be celebrated on that Sunday'.

'The Baptism of Christ' is a new festival in the Church

of England, though the readings in the ASB gave that theme to The First Sunday after Epiphany. The festival is kept on this day in the Roman calendar. CLC 2000 provides for this festival to be celebrated on the first Sunday of Epiphany (which takes the name of the festival, not the name of the Sunday). There is one exception to this rule. When 6 January is a Sunday and the Feast of the Epiphany itself is, in effect, the first Sunday of the Epiphany season, then the Baptism is celebrated on Monday 7 January. That will first happen in the year 2002. It is odd that this celebration, marking a key event in the Lord's self-understanding, a day of profound theological significance, should not have featured in the calendar in the past, and the addition of The Baptism of Christ to the list of festivals will be widely welcomed.

Later in the Epiphany season comes Christian Unity Week. There are collects and readings provided for this period. At the end of it comes The Conversion of St Paul. On Sundays of Epiphany, a festival may be transferred to the Monday, but may be kept on the Sunday, and the story of Paul's conversion sits very happily among Epiphany stories of the revelation of Christ to the world. Lectionary Note 6 requires that, when only two readings are used on this day at the principal service, Acts 19.1–22, the account of the conversion, be one of them.

THE PRESENTATION OF CHRIST

February 2 has no less than three titles widely used in the West: 'The Presentation of Christ in the Temple', 'The Purification of The Blessed Virgin Mary', and 'Candlemas', to which can be added, in the East, a fourth, 'The Meeting of our Lord'. *The Book of Common Prayer* uses the first two of these, but through much of Anglican history until recently it seems to have been the second, 'The Purification', that has had prominence and the day thought of as a festival of Mary, rather than of her Son. All recent calendar revisions have reserved that and made it as clear as possible that this is principally a feast of the Lord, though of course his mother has a significant place in the story of the day. February 2 celebrates that event, recorded in Luke 2.22–40, where the forty-day-old Jesus is taken by Joseph and Mary to the Temple for his presentation and her purification, where they are greeted by old Simeon and Anna, and where prophetic words are spoken about the suffering of both the son and his mother.

As a festival, the Presentation has often suffered from being detached from Christmas and Epiphany. Although only forty days on from 25 December, there has been a 'sea of green' between them and the incarnation has often seemed to have been packed up and put away for another year quite early on in January. The Presentation has not seemed to look back, let alone to look forward, but simply to be a rather isolated festival, a bit of colour in a dreary time of the year.

The Promise of His Glory determined to rescue The Presentation from that irrelevance, drew strongly on the tradition of an incarnation season of forty, rather than twelve, days, right up till 2 February, and also looked creatively at the place of The Presentation in relation to the whole liturgical cycle. It noted that, surprising as it might at first seem, this joyful feast day had long had a penitential note to it, with a tradition of purple as the liturgical colour for the procession, and that in reality the day has a bitter-sweet element to it: joy in the Lord 'suddenly coming to his temple' and hailed as the 'light of the nations and the glory of Israel' (leading to the custom of carrying candles and to the name 'Candlemas'), but seriousness because, of course, he comes in judgement, and sorrow because he is declared to be 'a sign that will be rejected' and that a sword will pierce his mother's soul too. It built on that and made The Presentation a pivotal point in the Christian year, the last look back through Epiphany to Christmas and then a turning to face in another direction; with Lent near (in some years very near indeed) to turn towards the passion. Understood like that the Presentation becomes a key moment in the liturgical cycle.

The Promise of His Glory made rich liturgical provision to allow The Presentation to be that key moment. CLC 2000 goes with that insight, not least in providing John 2.18–22 ('Destroy this temple and in three days I will raise it up again') as a reading at Evening Prayer. In time the Liturgical Commission in its *Book of Times and Seasons* will no doubt reproduce and refine the liturgical material now available for the Presentation, which ends with a procession of candles to the font and a text that gives expression to that turning from birth to passion. Meanwhile CLC 2000, following the logic of The Presentation as a key moment, makes it one of the nine Principal Feasts, and, to ensure its adequate celebration, allows its transfer from 2 February to the Sunday between 28 January and 3 February. If this is a pivotal day and a turning point, it needs to be one in which all the faithful share. If they will come on 2 February, all the better. But, if necessary, a transfer to the Sunday will make for a better observance and ensure that all will hear this lovely and profound tale of the old people, Anna (whom the ASB suppressed in the Gospel story, but CLC 2000 restores) and Simeon, who meet with the Lord in the temple, and will in turn be moved on in their thinking to be ready for Lent.

What CLC 2000 does not permit is a double celebration, The Presentation on a Sunday and also on 2 February. For, if that feast marks a fairly dramatic turning around in a new direction, it would be quite inappropriate to come back to church next day and find that nothing had changed and, a few days later, to go through the same dramatic turning all over again.

5

'Before Lent'

Between Candlemas and Ash Wednesday is a non-seasonal time of variable length. Very rarely (as in the year 2000) it will have as many as five Sundays, sometimes (as in 2002 and 2005) only one, but usually two or three. CLC 2000 is careful not to call this a 'Before Lent Season', for it prefers to see this time and the much longer time after Pentecost as 'non-seasonal'. It calls these two periods 'ordinary', as opposed to 'seasonal', time. It does not suggest that 'ordinary time' should give its name to the Sundays – 'The First Sunday of Ordinary Time' has little appeal – but it finds in the phrase 'ordinary time' a useful shorthand for describing these non-seasonal periods. The note on Ordinary Time reads:

> Ordinary Time is the period after the Feast of the Presentation of Christ until Shrove Tuesday and from the day after the Feast of Pentecost until the day before the First Sunday of Advent. During Ordinary Time, there is no seasonal emphasis.

There is no point searching for an underlying 'flavour' to these weeks between Candlemas and Ash Wednesday, for they do not have one, though the last two Sundays have a character of their own described below. The liturgical colour is green and that implies a neutrality where people can have time out from a developing drama and where local themes may have a chance to come to the fore.

After the last service of Candlemas (whether on 2 February or on the Sunday between 28 January and 3 February), the last vestiges of Christmas and Epiphany need to disappear immediately. Next morning is green and 'ordinary time' has taken over. CLC 2000 orders that the weekdays from then until the next Sunday always use the collect and post communion for The Fifth Sunday before Lent (even in the very rare year when The Fifth Sunday will be the *following* Sunday) and, more commonly, when the following Sunday will be the Third or Second Sunday before Lent.

As the last chapter explained, it is in these Sundays of Ordinary time before Lent that weeks can be lost or gained depending on the date of Easter. Five Sundays are provided for and named 'The Fifth, 'The Fourth', 'The Third' and 'The Second' Sundays before Lent and then 'The Sunday next before Lent'. Theoretically there might be no Sundays between The Presentation and Lent, for Ash Wednesday can be as early as 4 February, but in the first quarter of the next century, this will happen only once, in the year 2008. Equally five Sundays before Lent will be rare, though the year 2000 has five.

Inevitably this is the period of the year when the lectionary has least sense of direction or continuity. Because it is such an elastic period of time, the Sunday lections need to stand almost on their own from week to week. For the fifth, fourth and third Sundays, the lectionary operates as it does after Trinity, with readings attached to dates (i.e. 'Proper 2, Sunday between 10 and 16 February [if earlier than 2 before Lent]'), but collects attached to Sunday names. It is complicated, though fortunately the publishers of annual lectionaries and diaries will sort it out year by year and local clergy will not themselves have the task. But, as was explained in chapter 2, it was the only way to have at the same time collects attached to Sunday titles and readings that stayed with *The Revised Common Lectionary* and therefore with other churches.

It applies only to those three Sundays and not to the following two because of the provision in CLC 2000 to treat the two Sundays before Lent rather differently.

The Second Sunday before Lent is, in effect, a 'Creation Sunday'. CLC 2000 does not call it that; it retains its usual Sunday name. But it does ensure that, at a time when there are concerns with creation, and a desire to see them theologically, the Church has an opportunity, distinct from the rather different approach at Harvest Thanksgiving, to focus on this issue. Some will regret the passing of the ASB's Ninth Sunday before Christmas, not because they welcomed the cycle of themes it began, but because it served to focus on creation, and this can be a substitute for that. It brings it back to a period of the year that has had this emphasis in the past, for the Prayer Book tradition, though not its eucharistic readings, identified this theme with Septuagesima. It is the one Sunday where CLC 2000 has entirely abandoned *The Revised Common Lectionary* and one of very few where it has opted for a clear thematic approach. The collect and post communion prayer also go with the theme.

On the following Sunday, The Sunday Next Before Lent, *The Revised Common Lectionary* has two options; one continues with the semi-continuous Scripture reading with no thematic element (genuine 'ordinary time'), but the other makes this essentially a 'Transfiguration Sunday'. This is in itself an alternative to the use of Transfiguration material on the Second Sunday of Lent. CLC 2000 has rethought this series of options and gone for the Transfiguration readings on the Sunday Next before Lent without other choice. Again the collect and post communion prayer reflect the theme. There is a strong case for a remembrance of the Transfiguration at this point in the year, when the Lord comes down from the mountain and sets his face resolutely for Jerusalem, as well as for the more straightforwardly festal celebration on 6 August. But having this celebration in Lent (worst of all on Lent 4, conflicting with Mothering Sunday, as the ASB does) does not give it the chance that this new date will provide in leading people on towards the keeping of Lent.

So this otherwise neutral period begins to move people, via creation and transfiguration, towards the celebration of redemption. It is a natural progression.

6

Lent and Passiontide

THE FORTY DAYS OF LENT

The season of Lent prepares the Church for the celebration of the death and resurrection of the Lord. With its origins in the preparation of catechumens for their baptism at Easter and of those who had been excommunicated, for their readmission to sacramental life, and its development as a period of discipline and self-denial for all Christian people, it is a season that looks forward and presses on. It is not static, but dynamic, and though there is an important change of gear on The Fifth Sunday of Lent, when Passiontide begins, the whole of Lent builds towards Holy Week and the Passion. It is not, despite much misunderstanding, for which the hymn 'Forty days and forty nights' has much to answer, an historical reconstruction of the Lord's forty days in the wilderness. Admittedly that story is appointed as the Gospel reading in all three years in the lectionary provision for The First Sunday in Lent, but it is there simply as illustrative of the kind of discipline and self-denial required of the Christian, rather than because it has the same relationship to the season as, say, the resurrection narratives to Easter. Lent is about preparation for what comes at its climax; in a sense it has no theme, no major story, of its own.

A note states that 'The weekdays of Lent and every Friday in the year are days of discipline and self-denial, except all principal feasts and festivals and Fridays from Easter Day to Pentecost'. In other words, just as every

Friday in the year is a reminder of the cross, so every day in Lent has that quality also. We fast or impose on ourselves some other discipline because the cross is there ahead of us, drawing us on.

The liturgical colour of Lent (until the eve of Palm Sunday) is given as purple, and a note recognizes that that may vary from 'Roman purple' to violet, with blue as an alternative. Further, 'a Lent array of unbleached linen is sometimes used as an alternative to purple'.

Ash Wednesday, the first day of Lent, is one of three principal holy days (the others are Maundy Thursday and Good Friday) that stand alongside the nine principal feasts in the first category of observance. In effect, nine feasts and three fasts, a full dozen days. As with the principal feasts, it is noted that, under canon law, a celebration of the Holy Communion is required in every cathedral or parish church, except where there is dispensation under Canon B14A. *Lent, Holy Week, Easter* (SPCK, 1986) provides the commended service forms for Ash Wednesday, with the blessing and imposition of ashes, and this will in time be revised in the projected *Book of Times and Seasons.* The Ash Wednesday collect, as has been noted above, may be used from The First Sunday of Lent until Passiontide as the post communion prayer and this brings a unity and cohesion to this whole period.

The Sundays *of* Lent are so called, in preference to the Prayer Book and ASB's '*in* Lent', but this represents only a desire for consistency through the year; there is no deeper meaning in the change. The Third, Fourth and Fifth Sundays of Lent have, in Year A, a series of three very long Gospels from John. They are exceptionally long and in some places would need special treatment in terms of drama, or be divided into parts with singing or silence between the parts. It would be a pity simply

to shorten them. They are only provided for three
Sundays in three years, and the stories make their impact
for being heard in their entirety. They may provide
suitable occasions for a short homily, rather then a long
sermon. When it is desired to use all three and the second ('the man born blind') fits ill with Mothering Sunday,
a lectionary note allows the transfer of the principal lectionary readings to the second service on that day.

The Fourth Sunday in Lent raises questions beyond
that of Gospel length, for it is also Mothering Sunday,
which has its own set of demands in many churches,
and provides opportunities not to be missed in reaching
the wider community. Here CLC 2000 is as helpful as it
can be. It provides a collect and post communion prayer
for Mothering Sunday and a series of lections. The
Gospel reading is either Simeon's warning to Mary of
the sword to pierce her soul (Luke 2.33–35) or Mary at
the foot of the cross (John 19.25–27). The intention is
clear; it is to recognize Mothering Sunday and to make
provision for it, but in such a way that it does not detract
from, or cut across, the spirit of Lent, but continues the
momentum towards the Passion.

As with Advent, so also with Lent, CLC 2000 seeks an
observance of the season that will not suffer from too
many holy days that interrupt the spirit of the season. It
was that consideration that caused the Roman calendar
to move St Matthias from 24 February to 14 May, where
the story of his appointment can be read near Ascension
Day where it belongs in the post-Easter narratives. The
ASB went with that move and CLC 2000 stays with it,
while allowing by note the Prayer Book date of 24
February.

The Commission's proposals tried hard to move other
commemorations out of Lent; Cuthbert, for instance, to
4 September, the date of his translation, and now his

date in the Roman calendar, or Bishop Edward King to 3 June, the date of the Lincoln Judgement. However, both were returned to their traditional date by the Revision Committee (Edward King on 8 March and Cuthbert on 20 March) after spirited campaigns led from Lincoln and Durham, though a note still allows Cuthbert on 4 September, in line with Rome. Yet it remains the case that not every lesser festival has to be celebrated as such, and the calendar can be kept quite bare through Lent. In any case the feasts of martyrs, of whom there are several in Lent – Janani Luwum, Polycarp, Perpetua and Felicity, Thomas Cranmer – point to the cross as effectively as any way of keeping the season.

St Joseph of Nazareth (19 March) and The Annunciation of Our Lord to the Blessed Virgin Mary (25 March) fall usually in Lent. If they come in Holy Week, or indeed in Easter Week, they are transferred beyond the Second Sunday of Easter. The Annunciation, like the Presentation, is first and foremost a feast of the Lord, even if it is popularly called 'Lady Day'. CLC 2000, in line with canon law, makes it one of the nine principal feasts. But, because it falls in Lent, Sunday observance is not allowed and the note reads:

> These (principal feast) days, and the liturgical provision for them, may not be displaced by any other celebration, except that the Annunciation, falling on a Sunday, is transferred to the Monday following or, falling between Palm Sunday and the Second Sunday of Easter inclusive, is transferred to the Monday after the Second Sunday of Easter.

A similar note about St Joseph allows for the possibility of both the Annunciation and St Joseph being transferred beyond Easter Day, in which case St Joseph moves a day beyond the Annunciation. This will first happen in 2008.

Lent and Passiontide

PASSIONTIDE

The Fifth Sunday in Lent marks a significant change in Lent. It is often popularly called 'Passion Sunday', though this name appears in neither *The Book of Common Prayer* nor the ASB. It did appear in the *Proposed Prayer Book of 1928*. The difficulty is that it is the sixth Sunday of Lent that is *the* Sunday of the Passion, compounded by the fact that Roman calendar does indeed call Lent 6 'Passion Sunday', while Anglicans call it 'Palm Sunday'. Faced with this, CLC 2000 opts to use the name 'Passion Sunday' about neither day. It remains 'The Fifth Sunday of Lent'. Nevertheless the calendar adds 'Passiontide begins'. Lent is not over, but Passiontide adds another stratum, and the cross is closer. It is parallel with what we shall discover in relation to the nine days between Ascension and Pentecost, where Easter is not over, but new themes have been added. The changes on The Fifth Sunday of Lent come through the tone of collect and lections, through the replacement, if it has been used up till now as the post communion prayer, of the Ash Wednesday collect by something more directly relating to the passion, by a change in the hymnody to Passiontide provision, and in some churches by the veiling of crosses, statues and pictures.

The liturgical colour does not change at this point, but continues to be purple or Lent array, until Palm Sunday when red, the colour both of blood and of kingship, replaces it through Holy Week. The one exception is the Eucharist of the Last Supper on Maundy Thursday, for which white is the usual colour. On Good Friday and Easter Eve, it is customary to have the holy table bare, but on Good Friday the liturgical colour for the liturgy is red. The tradition of ministers in black and unsurpliced choirs does not adequately celebrate the triumph of the cross in the way the Good Friday liturgy intends.

Through Holy Week, the Church is well served by the liturgical provision of *Lent, Holy Week, Easter*, and in particular by the full liturgical forms provided there for Palm Sunday, for Maundy Thursday and for Good Friday. Maundy Thursday and Good Friday are, of course, principal holy days, but the notes hold back from saying about Good Friday what they say about every other principal feast or holy day, namely that the Eucharist is to be celebrated, because of the tradition that either abstains from communion on that day or receives from the elements set aside the previous night at the Eucharist of the Last Supper.

There are some important points to note in relation to the lectionary in Holy Week. Firstly, the Palm Sunday provision for the principal service divides into 'Liturgy of the Palms' and 'Liturgy of the Passion'. The intention here is not two separate occasions, but that the dynamic of the Palm Sunday liturgy is such that it leads from one into the other and that, because it is the Sunday of the Passion, we should not go home until we have been moved on from the story of the palm-waving crowds into the experience of the death of the Lord. It is the passion reading that we need to carry with us through Holy Week. There is therefore a need, even if it means shortening it in some pastoral settings, to see that the passion reading is not left out in favour of palms, processions and donkeys.

The principal service lectionary tackles the reading of the passion story by providing two in each year. On Good Friday invariably there is John's account. On Palm Sunday one of the synoptics is used, the one appropriate to that year. If it is 'the year of Mark', it will be the passion according to Mark. It would be pointless, staying with one evangelist through the year, to abandon him at this crucial moment. But where there is a tradition of singing the passion, there is a need to look ahead and look for suitable settings of Mark and Luke, and not always to fall back on Matthew, for which there is larger musical provision.

CLC 2000, unlike both the Prayer Book and the ASB, does not provide passion readings across the three (or four) weekdays after Palm Sunday. Shorter Gospels that introduce other elements of the Holy Week story are probably better on these days.

The lectionary notes for Good Friday allow some deviation from the second and third service lectionaries to ensure that the whole of the passion according to John is heard. If it is all read or sung at the Liturgy, then the 'second service lectionary' provides Colossians 1.18–23 and the 'third service lectionary' Hebrews 10.1–10. But the note makes these alternative to 'a part of John 18–19 if not read at the principal service'. This requires local decision, but it is obviously wise that, if the John Passion at the Liturgy has not started as early as the trial, it is appropriately read at Morning Prayer and, if it has not extended as far as the Burial, that should be read at Evening Prayer.

The lectionary provides some readings for use before the Easter Vigil. There is a firm tradition of not celebrating the Eucharist on the morning of Easter Eve and even one of having no offices, so that there is a sense of emptiness and waiting liturgically, reflecting the Lord's sojourn among the dead. But in some settings readings will be needed for public worship. The key fact is that the Easter Vigil, at whatever time after dark on Easter Eve or early on Easter Day it is celebrated, belongs to the Easter season. The CLC 2000 provision for 'Easter Eve' is for services earlier in the day, before the vigil, where it is the Lord in the tomb that is the theme, not the Lord whom the tomb could not contain.

7

Easter Day to Pentecost

EASTER

'The paschal character of the Great Fifty Days of Eastertide, from Easter Day to Pentecost, should be celebrated throughout the season, and should not be displaced by other celebrations.' Thus begins the CLC 2000 note on Eastertide. What is being asserted here is both the unique place of Eastertide in the Christian year and also the unity of the whole period from Easter Day to the Day of Pentecost. It does not always appear to be so. Easter can seem to be just another season; but it is the oldest period of celebration and its seven weeks are a sustained high point in the Christian year which no other time, not even the twelve days of Christmas, can match. Sometimes churches seem to tire very quickly of their celebration of the resurrection. Within two or three weeks of Easter Day, there has been a return to a 'normality' which Ascension Day and Whitsunday interrupt only momentarily.

In this respect some blame has to be taken by *The Book of Common Prayer*. Influenced by the medieval calendar, it makes something of the Monday and Tuesday of Easter Week, orders a proper preface at Holy Communion for only eight days, and soon settles back into collects and readings with little paschal character. Some time later comes Ascension Day, again with its 'octave' and then Whitsunday, with a mini-season of seven days before Trinity Sunday. There is little sense of the integrity of the whole fifty days from

Easter Day to Pentecost. The ASB begins to take it on board, with its distinctive Easter Greeting, Invitation to Communion and Dismissal and with its more paschal collects and readings, but still there is a sense of time 'after Easter' and of Ascension and Pentecost as separate seasons.

What CLC 2000 enjoins, and which is in line with the Roman calendar, is a much older tradition. It owes more, in scriptural terms, to Johannine chronology than its Lucan equivalent. Luke has the Lord ascend forty days after the resurrection and the Spirit given ten days later than that. John has a more complex picture in which resurrection, ascension and giving of Spirit overlap and integrate, like new strata added one by one. CLC 2000 goes firmly with this. Easter Day inaugurates a fifty day period, celebrating the 'Easter mystery', beginning with the resurrection of the Lord, with lections that draw that out, adding, on the fortieth day, the dimension of the ascension, and then preparing through the last nine days for the Day of Pentecost, which is both the last day of Eastertide and the celebration of the last part of the jigsaw, the gift of the Spirit. The calendar, supported by lectionary and collects, intends that this paschal character shall be sustained throughout the fifty days. *Lent, Holy Week, Easter* provided only a little liturgical material with which to do this, but *Enriching the Christian Year* and *Patterns for Worship* both supplement it considerably.

To say that Easter Day itself is one of the nine principal feasts is to understate its place in the year. It is the 'feast of feasts' and the 'queen of festivals'. It is the only named day in the year when communicant members of the Church of England are bound to receive Holy Communion. Like Christmas, it is not anticipated on its eve, which has its own provision. There is no 'First

Evening Prayer'. The transition from cross to resurrection lies in the Easter Liturgy.

In the Easter Liturgy, often known as the 'Vigil', though it is much more than that, the Church moves through a vigil of Scripture, silence and song, on to the kindling of light, the lighting of the paschal candle and the proclamation of the resurrection, next to a baptismal liturgy, and finally to the Eucharist in which the faithful are reunited with their risen Lord. When it is celebrated is a pastoral matter. It needs to be when the Church can assemble. That may be after dark on Saturday night. It may be at midnight. It may be as dawn breaks. It may be in the full light of the morning. There is something ideal about a celebration that can begin in darkness and end in light, but that will not make sense in every community. Providing that darkness has fallen on Easter Eve, and in Jewish terms the third day has begun, the Liturgy can also begin. But it is not an Easter Eve service, any more than the Christmas midnight mass is a Christmas Eve service. It is the beginning of a new season. It is resurrection time. What will not do is the kind of service that leaves worshippers uncertain whether Easter has begun or not. Once the candle has been lit and the resurrection proclaimed, one cannot step back into the night awaiting an Easter some hours ahead. It may well be that the first disciples found the empty tomb as dawn was breaking, but the decisive divine activity belonged to the night. That is theologically important. In the darkness God acted.

The principal service lectionary provides for the Easter 'Vigil' nine Old Testament readings, together with Romans 6 affirming the relationship between baptism and resurrection, and the appropriate Gospel account of the resurrection. The full set of Old Testament readings is unlikely to be used in many churches, and the notes require only three, one of which must be Exodus 14, the account of the escape from Egypt.

There is another set of readings for Easter for use during the day, with alternatives, and the possibility of reading the Johannine account as an alternative to the synoptic Gospel in any year. It also gives priority to Acts 10.34–43 (Peter speaking of the resurrection to Cornelius and his family), which must be read as the first or second reading. It is the first example of the provision from *The Revised Common Lectionary* of the Acts of the Apostles as the first reading, in place of the Old Testament, through the Easter season. It needs to begin on Easter Day if it is to serve as one of the distinctive characteristics of the season. But allowance has been made for any who see a real need to read the Old Testament each week, by ordering the Easter Vigil readings into a sequence that allows the use of one each Sunday through until Pentecost.

The calendar lists each of the weekdays of Easter Week on a par with Sundays and the Easter note already quoted continues: 'Except for a patronal or dedication festival, no festival may displace the celebration of Sunday as a memorial of the resurrection, and no saint's day may be celebrated in Easter Week'.

The numbering of the Sundays in Eastertide is important. It will come as no surprise that CLC 2000 insists that they are Sundays '*of* Easter', rather than 'after Easter'. The sense of 'after Easter' is the very thing the calendar is trying to avoid. But it is not as simple as with, say, Epiphany. For, whereas the Second Sunday of Epiphany is also the Second Sunday after Epiphany, the *Second* Sunday of Easter is the *First* Sunday after Easter. This will take time to get used to, and will be awkward for those also using the Prayer Book calendar. The fact the Commission and the Revision Committee were prepared to promote this calendrical variant, over and against the usual policy of going with Prayer Book titles, indicates the strength of feeling that the integrity of Eastertide needed to be strongly affirmed. The provision of collects with a clear paschal tone and the removal of several Prayer Book collects from this period is part of the same insistence, though the restoration of the Prayer Book's collect for The First Sunday after Easter (now the Second Sunday of Easter) is a welcome return of a fine text excluded from the ASB:

> Almighty Father,
> you have given your only Son to die for our sins
> and to rise again for our justification:
> grant us so to put away
>   the leaven of malice and wickedness
> that we may always serve you
> in pureness of living and truth;
> through the merits of your Son . . .

It has already been noted that the festivals of saints cannot be kept on Sundays in Eastertide nor in Easter Week. A further part of the note adds that 'the paschal character of the season should be retained on those weekdays when saints' days are celebrated. There are rules for transferring festivals that might fall in Easter Week or on a Sunday (St George, St Mark, St Philip & St James, and St Matthias) to the following Monday, and, if St George and St Mark are both transferred out of Easter Week (as will happen in 2000 and 2003) to move St George to the Monday and St Mark to the Tuesday. The important thing when keeping saints' days is, as the note implies, not to lose the special paschal flavour – Easter Greeting and Dismissal and many alleluias.

This also applies to the Rogation Days, the three days before Ascension Day, retained as days when prayer is offered for God's blessing on the fruits of the earth and human labour. The ASB lections for these days are retained and there are three collects, one concerned with the fruit of the land, one with industry, and one newly composed more general collect, related to the whole of human labour.

ASCENSION TO PENTECOST

It is in relation to Ascension Day and Pentecost that the biggest adjustment needs to be made by those used to the Prayer Book calendar or even that of the ASB. *The Book of Common Prayer* assumes an Ascension season of ten days, eight of them as an Ascension 'octave' and then, a few days later a Whitsun season of one week. *The Alternative Service Book* also assumed a ten-day Ascension season, signalled the end of Eastertide on Pentecost evening, nevertheless retained a week of Whitsun readings, and then conveyed to some by its lectionary choices the mistaken impression that the whole summer was an extended season of the Spirit.

CLC 2000 is very clear. There are four basic principles. Firstly, Ascension Day is a single day, a principal feast, not a season. Secondly, the nine days between Ascension Day and Pentecost are part of Eastertide, but prepare for Pentecost. Thirdly, Pentecost is both the feast of the Holy Spirit and the last day of Eastertide, bringing the Fifty Great Days to an end. Fourthly, the next day, the Monday after Pentecost, is 'ordinary time', a return to green as the liturgical colour. Each of these four principles needs spelling out a little more, though the last of them will wait for the next chapter for further clarification.

Ascension Day is a single day, forty days after Easter

Day. It is one of the nine principal feasts. Unlike some of them it cannot be transferred to a Sunday. It is not the end of anything, least of all of Eastertide. Nor is it a feast of an absenting Lord, for Jesus speaks of being with his disciples to the end of time, and the quaint, if slightly farcical, ceremony of extinguishing the paschal candle after the Gospel says all the wrong things about his continuing presence among his people. It is a day that marks the end of one kind of appearance and presence, but only after it had given way to another, and it celebrates his being with his Father, at his right hand, making intercession for us. There is also the sense that 'man with God is on the throne', in Christopher Wordsworth's phrase. But it is not about absence; it is another layer to the Easter mystery. Acts 1.1–11 is the key scriptural passage, which must be read at the principal service, but there is a rich variety of theological imagery behind it.

Traditionally reflection on these continues on the Sunday following. CLC 2000 does not do this (though the collect still hints at it), but instead allows the same ideas to be celebrated from a different angle at the end of the year on the Feast of Christ the King (see chapter 9). So what is lost here is gained there.

The second principle is that the nine days between Ascension and Pentecost are part of Eastertide, but prepare for Pentecost. The CLC 2000 Easter note reads: 'The nine days after Ascension Day until Pentecost are days of prayer and preparation to celebrate the outpouring of the Spirit.' It will need further work in a new daily office book and in the *Book of Times and Seasons* to fill this out with adequate liturgical provision, but the aim is clear. Pentecost is not a feast at which we should arrive unprepared and then start saying in the liturgy 'Come, Holy Spirit', as we do in the Pentecost hymns, through the days *after* it. 'Come, Holy Spirit' is what we should be singing and praying in the nine days that *lead up to* it, so that the feast itself becomes not only a remembering of the first Pentecost, but also a renewal of the outpouring of the Spirit in the Church. The nine days are a Pentecost sub-season within Eastertide, rather as Passiontide is a sub-season within Lent. That is indicated by the fact the Sunday within it is called 'The Seventh Sunday of Easter' – the alleluias of Easter continue and the paschal candle still burns.

The third principle is that the Day of Pentecost, Whitsunday, itself is both the climax of the nine-day Pentecost sub-season and the last day of Eastertide. The Acts 2.1–21 reading, which is mandatory at the principal service, sets the feast within its historic context in the pouring out of the Holy Spirit upon the Church, but, if the preparation has been thorough, people will be open to the power of that same Spirit today. But, because the gift of the Spirit is the last part of the Easter mystery, the final layer, Pentecost is also the final day of the whole season. With Evening Prayer on the Day of Pentecost, Easter comes to an end. The alleluias cease. The Easter greeting is no longer used. The paschal candle is extinguished. The post communion prayer expresses it like this:

> Faithful God,
> who fulfilled the promises of Easter
> by sending us your Holy Spirit
> and opening to every race and nation
> the way of life eternal:
> open our lips by your Spirit,
> that every tongue may tell of your glory;
> through Jesus Christ our Lord.

8

'*After Trinity*'

This chapter takes its title from the fact that the Sundays through the summer have been named 'after Trinity', but the period of time to which it refers begins, not after Trinity Sunday itself, but a week earlier on the Monday after the Day of Pentecost. For that day marks a return to the non-seasonal Ordinary time described in chapter 5. Before Lent there is a comparatively short period of Ordinary time. Now comes the much longer period stretching through to the end of the liturgical year. Its liturgical colour is green, its reading of Scripture is semi-continuous, its collects are general, rather than seasonal, and it stands in contrast to the seasons with their very clear focus and direction.

CLC 2000 provides a collect and post communion prayer for use 'on the weekdays after the Day of Pentecost', to begin on that Monday morning, in order that there is a sense of new beginning, with Pentecost left behind, rather than a 'week of the Spirit' that is not quite Ordinary time.

But two important celebrations come early in this period of Ordinary Time. The first is Trinity Sunday, one of the nine principal feasts, with full provision and no possibility of anything taking precedence over it. *Enriching the Christian Year* gives additional liturgical material to enhance this feast and the *Book of Times and Seasons* will no doubt do the same. Although the 'after Trinity' Ordinary Time has green as its liturgical colour, this feast day has white (or gold). But it has no 'octave' or mini-season and next day, another Monday morning, returns to green.

The second celebration is on the following Thursday. Listed among the festivals, a note says 'The Thursday after Trinity Sunday may be observed as the Day of Thanksgiving for the Holy Communion (sometimes known as *Corpus Christi*), and may be kept as a festival'. The note seeks to cover a number of possibilities, necessary in a Church of England that is divided about this medieval festival. Some may not wish to keep it at all. No one requires them to do so; it is an optional observance. Some may wish to call it '*Corpus Christi*' and they may; other may prefer the more descriptive and intelligible, but less poetic, 'Day of Thanksgiving for the Holy Communion'. Some may wish to keep it as a lesser festival, others to give it the status of a festival. Both are permissable. To provide for those who wish to make the most of it, there are full sets of readings for Morning and Evening Prayer (including a First Evening Prayer) as well as for Holy Communion, and, of course, collect and post communion. CLC 2000 does not address the issue of what happens when this celebration, kept as a festival, collides with another (such as St Barnabas in 1998 or 2009). Logic suggests that, since *Corpus Christi*, is invariably the Thursday after Trinity Sunday, the other festival moves on a day.

The decision to name the Sundays through the summer 'after Trinity' was one made carefully and the Revision Committee received some submissions asking it to reverse the Commission's proposal. At one level not too much should be read into the name of the Sunday. 'After Pentecost' does not mean a season of the Spirit and 'after Trinity' does not mean a season of the Trinity. Here the word 'after', as opposed to 'of', is important. This is not the 'Trinity season'. It is Ordinary Time, but within Ordinary Time Sundays need names. The Roman 'Sunday of the Year' or 'Sunday of Ordinary Time' were rejected as prosaic and unattractive. The choice of a convenient name lay between 'after Trinity' and 'after Pentecost'.

The decision in the ASB to go for 'after Pentecost' was influenced by a number of factors. There was a strong claim for it as the ecumenical front runner. The Roman Catholic Church had long used this description of the summer Sundays. Other Anglican provinces and other denominations were doing the same. There was also a sense that the ASB eucharistic lectionary divided the year into three and the period after Pentecost focused on life within the Church, with an emphasis on the Book of Acts. It was indeed life 'after Pentecost'. It is probably not accurate to say that the decision was a response to the heightened awareness of the significance of the Holy Spirit in the life of the Church that the Charismatic Movement represents, for the proposed calendar change pre-dates that movement, but it would be true to say that in the 1960s and 1970s the doctrine of the Trinity failed to excite. The Church was not abandoning its Trinitarian faith, but it was not engaging much with the theology of the Trinity. 'After Pentecost' seemed more relevant and a refreshing change.

But in preparing CLC 2000, other factors prevailed. First there was the Commission's aim to stay with *The Book of Common Prayer* where possible. There was therefore a bias towards 'after Trinity' from the start. For here was the opportunity for the two calendars to be in step for nearly half the year. But beyond that the arguments that seemed strong twenty-five years before seemed weaker now. It was probably still correct that 'after Pentecost' was the strongest ecumenical contender, but it was no longer true that the Roman Catholic Church was using it. It was certainly no longer the case that the lectionary had a logic that gave the period after Pentecost an emphasis on the Spirit (though *The Revised Common Lectionary* at points assumed that 'after Pentecost' would appear in Sunday titles). It was also no longer the case that the Trinity was sidelined in theological thinking. There has been a flourishing of writing on the significance of the doctrine of the Trinity for Christian life and worship. To the Commission and to the Revision Committee, it was clear that the balance was in favour of 'after Trinity', which had been the distinctive use of the British Isles, following the Sarum use, through most of the last millennium.

The difficulty of attaching readings to named Sundays through this period has already been explored. The Church of England wants to be in step with other churches using *The Revised Common Lectionary*. It can only do that by using readings attached to calendar dates. Equally it wants to retain historic Sunday titles and collects attached to them. It cannot integrate these two things. The result is that, on the Third Sunday after Trinity, for instance, though the collect and post communion prayer will always be the same, the readings will vary. An annual lectionary will indicate the proper choices, though they be deduced from CLC 2000. Mention has also already been made (in chapter 2) of the two-track approach to the Old Testament in this period. The minister must choose each year between a track of Old Testament readings that reflect the Gospel of the day or a track that reads semi-continuously from Old Testament books quite independently of the other lections.

There are no restrictions on keeping festivals on Sundays. The Roman calendar will not allow this, except in the case of a very few celebrations. CLC 2000 does permit it, but does not require it; these days may always be transferred to the Monday. There are, as often, contrary arguments. Saints' days on Sundays may be said to detract from the celebration of Sunday as the day of the resurrection and certainly interrupt the cycle of readings. On the other hand, it is a pity if the celebration of heroic sanctity is confined to weekdays with few people present, and sometimes the intrusion of a saint's day is a fresh stimulus after many weeks of green Sundays after Trinity.

To move to the other end of the period 'after Trinity', we find a difference between the Prayer Book and CLC 2000. For reasons that will emerge in the following chapter, the new calendar brings this period to an end at All Saints' Day. The last Sunday after Trinity in CLC 2000 is always the last Sunday in October (or 24 October when 31 October is a Sunday and kept as All Saints' Day). If there are Sundays to be omitted they are The Twenty-first, Twentieth, Nineteenth Sundays, and so on, rather than The Last Sunday after Trinity. On this day the collect is the one that the Prayer Book appoints for Advent 2 ('Blessed Lord, who hast caused all holy Scriptures to be written for our learning . . .) and that influenced the choice of that date as Bible Sunday. CLC 2000 moves Bible Sunday to this Last Sunday after Trinity, close to what in some denominations is 'Reformation Sunday' and provides the day also with a three-year cycle of alternative lections specifically for a Bible Sunday observance. It becomes therefore, like the two Sundays before Lent, one of those rare Sundays with a clear theme, though, in this case, if the ordinary readings for the day are preferred, the emphasis does not go much beyond the collect and the post communion prayer.

The hope has to be that other denominations and the Bible societies will be willing to relocate Bible Sunday on to this day and that it may be a genuinely ecumenical observance.

9

All Saints to Advent

MAKING SENSE OF NOVEMBER

CLC 2000 gives the weeks between All Saints' Day (1 November) and Advent a distinctive flavour of their own, but falls short of declaring them to be a season. It is quite clear that the start of the Christian cycle is Advent Sunday and that, even if the Sundays of this period are designated Sundays 'before Advent', they belong to the tail end of the year, not to its beginning, though in a cycle end always gives way to beginning. The key note in relation to this period is that on 'Ordinary Time'. It defines Ordinary Time as 'the period after the Feast of the Presentation of Christ until Shrove Tuesday, and from the day after the Feast of Pentecost until the day before the First Sunday of Advent. During Ordinary Time, there is no seasonal emphasis'. But it goes on to add immediately, 'except that the period between All Saints' Day and the First Sunday of Advent is observed as a time to celebrate and reflect upon the reign of Christ in earth and heaven'. Behind that note, which may seem to raise more issues than it resolves, lies a recent history of trying to make sense of November in the calendar of the Church of England.

The calendar of *The Alternative Service Book* gave the Church the 'nine Sundays before Christmas'. This was dictated partly by a desire for a longer Advent, so that important Advent themes should not be squeezed out by pre-Christmas celebrations. It was also influenced by

the lectionary shape, with its emphasis on the First
Person of the Trinity in the first part of the Christian
year. What was created was a lectionary and calendar
that began in late October and presented a whistle stop
tour of the Old Testament – with Creation, the Fall,
Abraham, Moses and the Faithful Remnant in a five-
week sequence, and then into Advent. Reflecting on it
later it may seem that this was not a good way to handle
the Old Testament and certainly it did not much meet
the need of an extended Advent in terms of exploring
the great Advent themes, which are much more concerned with the future than the past. But, even laying
those criticisms aside, the sequence was off to a bad start
beginning on a Sunday when many are on half-term
holiday and then immediately in conflict with other
observances at that time of the year. Its themes did not
marry well with either All Saintstide or Remembrance
Sunday. Those looking over their shoulder to the Roman
calendar also saw in 'Christ the King' a more compelling
theme for the Sunday next before Advent than 'the
Faithful Remnant'.

The Commission addressed this in preparing for
publication *The Promise of His Glory*. What struck the
Commission then was that the desire to anticipate
Advent themes in the weeks of November (which was
nothing novel, for the Ambrosian rite has a six-week
Advent and the Prayer Book's own collect and lections
for the last Sunday after Trinity have an Advent ring to
them) accorded well with the themes that were thrown
up naturally by All Saints, All Souls, Remembrance and
Christ the King. In a nutshell these themes were about
'the Kingdom'. They concerned the rule of Christ among
the saints in heaven, about the coming of that kingdom
on earth 'as it is in heaven', and about the relationship

of the authorities of this world to the rule of Christ. Bringing these together into a coherent season that rounded off the old year and led naturally into the new seemed the right way forward.

What emerged in *The Promise of His Glory* was this season of the Kingdom inaugurated on All Saints' Day and continuing to the very eve of Advent. All Saints' Day became for this part of the year the same pivotal day that the Presentation became earlier in the cycle. Instead of being an isolated feast day, it became a key moment of transition into a new season with its own themes and dynamic. The proposal was well received and given further credibility and seasonal texts in *Celebrating Common Prayer* and it was therefore not surprising that the Commission then stayed with the Kingdom option in its calendar, lectionary and collect report to the synod in 1995. It had been refined somewhat. It was now clearer still that this was an end season to the year, not an anticipatory beginning. *The Revised Common Lectionary* had been marginally revised to accentuate the Kingdom emphasis (though it hardly needed to be done, for the Roman Mass Lectionary has the same underlying theme, however much it may still be Ordinary time), and the collects and post communion prayers were given the same emphasis.

It was the part of the Commission's proposals about which the Revision Committee had most doubts. The Committee supported entirely the Commission's desire to abandon the ASB Nine Sundays approach, to make more of All Saintside and to bring a greater cohesion to these weeks of the year, but there were two reservations about the Kingdom season. The first was simply in its name. The term 'kingdom' has a wealth of meaning in the teaching of Jesus and more widely in the

Scriptures. There was a feeling that this was to define the kingdom too narrowly and to lose much of that wealth of meaning. There was a long search for another name for the season. But there arose a more fundamental worry about the creation of a new season at all. Despite the popularity of the Kingdom season as *The Promise of His Glory* and *Celebrating Common Prayer* had developed it, if the ASB's approach had worn thin so quickly, was there not a real danger that what was now being proposed would look equally dated within a generation? And was it right for the Church of England to go it almost alone in creating a new season when all its other instincts were to stay in step with other churches and other provinces?

The Revision Committee's solution is inevitably something of a compromise, but that was intentional, wishing to give much more time for the idea of a distinctive period in November to find its level. So, in the end, no new season has been created in CLC 2000 and Ordinary Time extended until the eve of Advent. But the Sundays are given the title 'Sundays before Advent', rather than continuing with the 'after Trinity' sequence; the lectionary and collect emphasis proposed by the Commission is retained, red (for kingship) is given as the preferred liturgical colour (but with a continuation of the green of Ordinary Time for those who prefer it), the note about this period as 'a time to celebrate and reflect upon the reign of Christ in earth and heaven' has been added, and the Sunday next before Advent given the title Christ the King. In other words, CLC 2000 goes down the path the Commission advocated, but without a Kingdom season. Time will tell whether the distinctiveness of this period takes hold of the Church or whether Ordinary Time wins the day.

SPECIAL DAYS FROM ALL SAINTS'
TO CHRIST THE KING

All Saints' Day is the last of the nine principal feasts of the year. A note allows its celebration 'on either 1 November or the Sunday falling between 31 October and 6 November; if the latter there may be a secondary celebration on 1 November'. There is some parallel with the way The Presentation is handled. Once again, here is a day considered so crucial to the cycle that it may be transferred to a Sunday so that all the faithful may share in it. But, unlike the Presentation, where a second celebration on a week day would undermine the sense of the feast as the final moment of the incarnation season, All Saints' may be kept both on 1 November and on the Sunday, and sufficient lections are provided to do this. If it is kept on the Sunday it is called 'All Saints' Sunday' and the All Saints' Day prayers and readings are used, with additional readings provided for 1 November. If it is kept only on 1 November, the main All Saints' Day provision is used on that day, and the Sunday after, called 'The Fourth Sunday before Advent', has different prayers and readings of its own.

November 2 is designated 'The Commemoration of the Faithful Departed (All Souls' Day)'. The longer title reflects an evangelical sensitivity in relation to prayer and the departed. Collect, post communion prayer and readings for the Eucharist are provided. The day has the status of a lesser festival. This means that those who do not wish to, need not celebrate it. But it is the kind of day that those who do celebrate it will probably want both to have readings for it at Morning and Evening Prayer and also not to lose it when it falls on a Sunday. Here the notes on lesser festivals come to the rescue. One such note allows the minister to draw from the provision for Holy Communion psalms and readings for use at Morning and Evening Prayer. November 2 has sufficient provision to do this. Another allows a day that would normally be omitted because it fell on a Sunday to be kept on the nearest available day. This would mean that in 2003 and 2008 All Souls' Day could be kept on Monday 3 November, as in 1997.

Remembrance Sunday, which is the Sunday nearest to 11 November, is celebrated unevenly across the land. In some places it remains an important milestone in the community's life; in others little liturgical provision is called for. CLC 2000 has provided readings that reflect on the relationship between the kingdom of God and the kingdoms of the world. These accord well with the concerns of Remembrance Sunday, while also being suitable in places where that emphasis is not needed. In addition the collect and post communion prayer for The Third Sunday before Advent (two rather fine prayers adapted from the ASB) also fit this concern, though there are a minority of years when Remembrance Day Sunday falls a week later, on the Second Sunday before Advent.

The final Sunday of the liturgical year is designated 'Christ the King' and has the status of a festival. It is a new observance in official Church of England provision. *The Revised Common Lectionary* proposed 'The Reign of Christ', that particular terminology possibly reflecting a North American suspicion of a male title. The Commission (following *The Promise of His Glory*) proposed 'The Kingship of Christ', but only as an optional festival, in much the same way as *Corpus Christi* is included. The hesitation was because this is a twentieth-century festival of Roman Catholic origin, and there was a worry lest it seem an improper importation into Anglicanism. But the Revision Committee, though it abandoned the

Kingdom as a season, was keen nevertheless to strengthen the kingdom emphasis on this particular day. It discovered that there was no suspicion of a 'Christ the King' festival, and, preferring a person to a concept, went for 'Christ the King' as the title and made it a mandatory festival. It provides a fitting christological climax to the liturgical year and its picture of Christ upon the throne leads naturally to Advent and to Christ as Judge.

There remains the question of the traditional collect of the Sunday next before Advent, beginning 'Stir up, we beseech thee . . .' It is well known, much loved, firmly associated with this day, and taken into folk culture in association with Christmas puddings. But it is not the obvious collect for Christ the King. The ASB made it an alternative to a 'faithful remnant' thematic collect, but also appointed it for another Sunday in October – too early for stirring puddings. CLC 2000's solution is to make it the post communion prayer at the Eucharist on its traditional day and through the following week, but also to suggest that it be used as the collect at Morning and Evening Prayer through the weekdays that follow. In this way Christ the King and 'Stir Up' Sunday can sit happily together.

10

Celebrating the Saints

SAINTS' DAYS IN THE CHURCH OF ENGLAND

In the sixteenth and seventeenth centuries the Church of England, unlike some churches of the Reformation, retained some liturgical commemoration of the saints. *The Book of Common Prayer* gives two categories of commemoration, often known as 'red-letter' and 'black-letter' saints (because of the colour of their entries in the calendar), and for the red-letter saints a collect, epistle and Gospel are provided. *The Proposed Prayer Book* of 1928 and *The Alternative Service Book* of 1980 both extend that commemoration, by adding new red-letter days, by commemorating additional saints and by providing sets of collects and readings for various common categories of saints – martyrs, teachers, bishops, etc. The ASB also broke new ground by including in its calendar a number of uncanonized heroes of the faith. It was not exactly 'making saints', for that is not the Church of England way, but it was recognising heroic sanctity in the calendar, neither more nor less.

CLC 2000 takes the celebration of saints and heroes of the faith a stage or two further. It has four categories of observance. The first, 'principal feasts', has already been fully described. Only one of them (All Saints' Day) is concerned with the celebration of the saints. Then come festivals, essentially the red-letter days in the old nomenclature. In the third category are the lesser festivals. In a fourth and new category are commemorations.

Not everybody is looking for rich provision for saints days. Strictly speaking principal feasts should by canon law always be marked by a celebration of Holy Communion and festivals by proper psalms, readings and collects at Morning and Evening Prayer, as a minimum. But all celebration of lesser festivals and commemorations is entirely optional, and the reality is that some churches, often through necessity, sit light even to festivals except when they fall on Sunday. But provision is not made to suit the minimum need, but to serve the needs of places where there is a full pattern of daily worship, and in cathedrals, religious communities and some parish churches every day needs provision for Morning and Evening Prayer and for the Holy Communion, and in these places people will often want quite a full (though not overloaded) calendar of the saints, backed up by a wide choice of appropriate liturgical material.

To the three categories not already described – festivals, lesser festivals and commemorations – we now turn.

FESTIVALS

In CLC 2000 festivals are days that are never omitted in any year, though sometimes they might be transferred from their normal day. For each of them there is full liturgical provision in terms of collect and post communion and of psalms and readings at Morning and Evening Prayer and at the Eucharist. There is no canonical requirement to celebrate Holy Communion, but no canonical permission to ignore their celebration at the daily office. Provision is almost made for a First Evening Prayer on the eve of the festival, but (unlike the provision for principal feasts) the use of this is optional. These days may, for most of the year, be celebrated on a Sunday when they fall on one, but not in Advent, Lent or Eastertide. In those seasons, and optionally at other times, they are transferred to the Monday.

There are twenty-eight such festivals in CLC 2000. Five of them are not festivals of saints, but of the Lord himself (his Naming and Circumcision, his Baptism, his transfiguration, Holy Cross Day and Christ the King). Of the other twenty-three, eighteen (most of them feasts of apostles and evangelists) are in the calendar of *The Book of Common Prayer*. The additional ones are St Mary Magdalene (22 July), which had been in the Prayer Book of 1549 and reappeared in 1928, St Joseph of Nazareth (19 March) and The Blessed Virgin Mary (for date, see below), which entered the calendar in 1980, and St George (23 April) and The Visit of the Blessed Virgin Mary to Elizabeth (31 May) which are new in CLC 2000.

The inclusion of St George, the early fourth-century Roman soldier turned Christian martyr, aroused more interest in the secular press than the rest of the calendar proposals put together. His day was not designated a festival in the Commission's original proposals, but the Revision Committee added him, declaring 'although we did not want to embrace a narrow sort of nationalism, we were convinced that the patron saint of England ought to be celebrated as a Festival by the Church of England'. In the Roman Calendar for England his day is a 'feast'.

The inclusion of the Visit of Mary to Elizabeth as a festival was part of a rethink of the place of Mary, the mother of the Lord, in the calendar. In the Prayer Book, both the Purification (2 February) and the Annunciation (25 March) are seen as festivals of Mary. We understand both of them now as principally feasts of the Lord himself. In the light of that the compilers of ASB 1980 proposed a celebration of her on 15 August, the day of a feast in her honour since the fourth century, later uniting both east and west. The proposal was not to celebrate any particular event, scriptural or otherwise, but to remember the totality of Mary's life, though the collect and readings proposed looked more towards her heavenly glory than her earthly life. But the General Synod at the time was persuaded to abandon that date, because of its association in the Roman Catholic Church with the doctrine of the assumption, and to opt instead for 8 September, traditionally the celebration of her 'nativity'. The ASB has therefore celebrated the beginning of her earthly life with collect and readings more suited to the end of it. Over the succeeding years few Anglican provinces have followed the lead of the Church of England, most of them opting for a festival of Mary on 15 August. In its 1995 proposals the Liturgical Commission recommended that England also adopt the 15 August date and the Revision Committee concurred. An attempt on the floor of the synod to reverse this received only a handful of votes and a further appeal to the House of Bishops did not move them to make a change. August 15 is therefore the date for the Festival of the Blessed Virgin Mary. But a note also allows that 'the festival of the Blessed Virgin Mary (15 August) may, for pastoral reasons, be celebrated instead on 8 September'. 'Pastoral reasons' might, of course, mean the inconvenience of a date in the middle of the holiday season or else the doctrinal unacceptability of the original date.

The Visit of Mary to Elizabeth has been made a festival, not so much because it honours Mary as because it recalls a fine New Testament story that plays its part in the incarnation cycle. The Annunciation to Mary, the Birth of John (the setting for Zechariah's song), The Presentation in the Temple (the setting for Simeon's song) each have their day. This story of shared faith and joy, the setting for Mary's song, belongs with them, and is rich in encouragement.

One other festival needs a comment. This is St Peter and St Paul on 29 June. The Prayer Book makes this a day of St Peter only. The ASB allowed either St Peter alone, as its first option, or St Peter and St Paul together, as an alternative. CLC 2000 simply reverses this. It gives St Peter and St Paul together, as the first option, with St Peter alone as the alternative. There was an attempt to reverse this in the General Synod. But the Synod accepted the argument for the double festival, since it was one of the oldest festivals in the Christian calendar, dating from AD 258 during the Valerian persecution in Rome. What had changed, it was argued, since 1980 was that a succession of Anglican provinces had restored the more ancient title to the day, leaving the Church of England increasingly isolated. This was not the kind of issue on which there was any virtue in standing alone. But there is still the alternative of Peter alone, for those who require it, and among them will be churches dedicated to Peter, but not to Paul. There is some overlap in the lections for the two ways of keeping the day, but the collect is necessarily different.

The lectionary provision for these festivals includes three eucharistic readings, though there will often only be two used. A note requires that, when there are only two, the first shall always, on the Conversion of St Paul and on the festivals of St Matthias, St Barnabas, St James and St Stephen, be the Acts reading because it is in Acts that we read about their life or their death. The eucharistic lections also follow *The Revised Common Lectionary* in treating readings from Acts and Revelation as the First Reading, followed by an Epistle, but always with an alternative approach that retains the Old Testament.

LESSER FESTIVALS

The note on 'lesser festivals' describes them in this way:

> Lesser festivals, which are listed in the calendar, are observed at the level appropriate to a particular church. Each is provided with a collect, psalm and readings, which may supersede the collect of the week and the daily eucharistic lectionary. The daily psalms and readings at Morning and Evening Prayer are not usually superseded by those for lesser festivals, but at the Minister's discretion psalms and readings provided on these days for the Holy Communion may be used at Morning and Evening Prayer. The Minister may be selective in the lesser festivals that are observed, and may keep some or all of them as 'commemorations'.

CLC 2000 was not breaking new ground by including in this category uncanonized heroes of the faith from the Anglican Communion and the Reformed Churches. This had been debated in the 1958 Lambeth Conference, is done in other provinces and is established in England through the 1980 calendar. Some did argue to the Revision Committee against this development, but the Committee responded thus:

> We faced the issue of how in the Anglican tradition, where we have no canonization procedure, names can be tested for inclusion in the calendar. We became more confident that the Holy Spirit has guided Anglican provinces in placing within their calendars many of our own Anglican saintly figures, people like George Herbert, Richard Hooker, John Keble and Edward King, and we set ourselves against too narrow a view of what constituted veneration or

'cult'. Especially in the modern world it is often difficult to locate evidence of a cult geographically, but it
is real nonetheless.

Against the background of this thinking, the
Commission and then the Revision Committee had to
examine hundreds of possible names for inclusion. In
the end the revision of the list of lesser festivals was a
fairly conservative one. It sought to redress some bal-
ances – more women, more lay people, more modern
'saints'. It abandoned the ASB's group commemorations
in favour of named individuals. It stuck by the con-
vention that no name should find a place among the
lesser festivals until the person had been dead for fifty
years ('the fifty year rule'), but made the exception of
martyrs, for the witness of martyrs to Christ is not by
the quality of their lives, but by the manner of their
death. It moved some entries to different dates to avoid
clashes and to clear Advent and Lent of too many
names.

Saints (some from the Prayer Book of 1662, some
from 1928), who had been removed in 1980 reappear,
among them Anskar, Alphege, Richard, Etheldreda,
Swithun, Monica, Ninian, Alfred, Leo, Clement, together
with the Beheading of John the Baptist. New entries
include Aelred of Hexham and Alcuin of York, Hilde-
gard of Bingen and Elizabeth of Hungary, Gregory of
Nyssa and Macrina his theologian sister, Henry Martyn,
Mary Sumner and, in our own time, Janani Luwum,
Archbishop of Uganda, martyred under the Amin regime
in 1977. The 'English Saints and Martyrs of the
Reformation Era' are celebrated on 4 May, the day the
Roman Church in England remembers its own martyrs
of that period.

For each of these days there is a collect of its own,
many of them newly written, with provision for a

post communion from a series of 'commons'. There are categories of readings, and particular ones noted as suitable for particular names in the calendar. *Exciting Holiness* (Canterbury Press, 1997) makes this material available in a form easy to use and supplements the official provision with a short 'hagiography' for liturgical use and a collection of writings about those named in the calendar or by them.

Lesser festivals when they fall on a Sunday or coincide with a movable feast or festival normally lapse. A note allows them to be retained and moved to the first free day if that would be helpful.

COMMEMORATIONS

The fourth category of observance is a 'commemoration'. In a sense, it is not unlike a 'black-letter day' of *The Book of Common Prayer*, for it is a name in the calendar, but without liturgical provision for it. The note explains:

> Commemorations, which are listed in the calendar, are made by a mention in prayers of intercession and thanksgiving. They are not provided with collect, psalm and readings, and do not replace the usual weekday provision at either the Holy Communion or Morning and Evening Prayer. The minister may be selective in the commemorations that are made.

Mentioning a name in the prayers and letting that lead into appropriate thanksgiving or intercession is very different from declaring someone to be a saint. As the Revision Committee put it, 'When people speak of inclusion among the Commemorations as tantamount to canonization they have entirely misunderstood the way the Church of England celebrates sanctity'.

The new category of commemorations allowed the Commission to put before the Synod a far larger number of holy men and women, without flooding the calendar with a lesser festival nearly every day. It saw the commemorations as a place to include some of the saints and heroes of every age not included in the lesser festivals. It was not that they were less holy, but that their stories had less immediate relevance to England or to the twentieth century. In the end a calendar has to be selective. Many of them have appeared in calendars, even Church of England calendars in the past. But the large majority of them were new to Church of England provision, quite a number of them from the twentieth century. Their inclusion may be seen as a 'first step', testing the water to see whether their stories inspire Christian people in their discipleship. If that turns out to be the case, some of them might be found in a later revision of the calendar among the lesser festivals.

These 'modern' commemorations represent a broad range of twentieth-century holiness. Oscar Romero, Dietrich Bonhoeffer and Maximilian Kolbe are among the martyrs of our time and Edith Cavell gave her life to save others in time of war. Charles Gore and Brooke Foss Westcott were among the great bishop-theologians of the century. Mary Slessor was a missionary in West Africa. Samuel Azariah and Sundah Singh in India, Apolo Kivebulaya in Central Africa and Ini Kopuria in Melanesia established the faith in their own countries. Charles de Foucauld established his brotherhood in the Sahara, and, rather differently, here in Britain William Booth founded the Salvation Army and Wilson Carlile the Church Army. Geoffrey Studdert Kennedy was a poet, as well as a remarkable army chaplain in war time, and Evelyn Underhill a writer and mystic. Isabella Gilmore pushed forward women's ministry in the

Church, and in their different ways Samuel and
Henrietta Barnett, Florence Nightingale, Octavia Hill
and Eglantine Jebb worked among the poor and called
the Church to social justice. William Temple brought
together the ministry of archbishop, theologian, philoso-
pher, ecumenist and social thinker in a remarkable way.
It is an impressive and, in the best sense, catholic list.

The Revision Committee made one important decision that altered considerably the Commission's list of
commemorations. The Commission had not applied the
'fifty year rule' to commemorations in the way that it
had to lesser festivals. But the Committee decided that
it was simply too soon to bring into the calendar those
who had died within a few years (except as martyrs)
and extended the fifty-year rule to this category. It
means that figures like Amy Carmichael, founder of the
Dohnavur Fellowship, who died in 1951, Paul Couturier,
worker for the Ecumenical Movement, who died in
1953, Pierre Teilhard de Chardin, scientist and visionary,
who died in 1955, and the Church of England's own
George Bell, Bishop of Chichester, who died in 1958,
must wait for inclusion until fifty years have passed.
Others from the 1960s and 1970s wait in the wings,
perhaps too early to be assessed.

It means that the Church of England needs a mechanism by which new names can be added to the calendar
at periods between its major revisions. The Commission
and the Revision Committee have both asked that the
House of Bishops bring forward a mechanism for doing
this.

But not all the names among the commemorations
are new ones. Some are very old names indeed, not
sufficiently significant in most churches to be included
among the lesser festivals, but important for some.
Among them will be the saints who give their names to

many parish churches, saints such as Margaret of Antioch, Giles of Provence and Catherine of Alexandria. The note on commemorations allows for such circumstances: 'A commemoration may be observed as a lesser festival, with liturgical provision from the common material for holy men and women, only where there is an established celebration in the wider church or where the day has a special local significance'. The collection of 'common' collects, post communions and sets of readings means that there always is the possibility of making more of these commemorations, but the tone of CLC 2000 is to discourage too much of it. The note ends with the warning: 'In designating a commemoration as a 'lesser festival', the Minister must remember not to lose the spirit of the season, especially of Advent and Lent, by too many celebrations that detract from its character'.

SAINTS AND THE LIFE OF THE CHURCH

The Church is encouraged and enriched by the celebration of its fellowship with its saints and heroes through the generations. In its report to the General Synod in 1995, the Liturgical Commission, in seeking to explain its criteria for inclusion in the calendar, quote in full a document prepared by Canon Brian Hardy for the Scottish Episcopal Church. Lest, in all this talk of categories and lists, the essential point be lost, it is worth concluding this chapter with part of that document that the Commission found helpful in its own work:

> When a Church decides on a list of those whom it wishes to commemorate in its worship, it is in fact making a statement about the way in which it understands its relationship to the universal Church, to the particular Communion of which it is part, and to the

country or culture in which it is set. There are at least four aspects to such a statement.

1. *Communion*
A recognition of the universal nature of the Body of Christ, and of the living fellowship of that divided Body across all frontiers of space, time and denomination.

2. *Inspiration*
Those are commemorated who stir us to renewed fellowship in the faith. They may be people around whom significant events have taken place in the story of the Church. They may be people in whose lives the light of Christ has shone, and who renew in us the sense of God's holiness.

3. *Reconciliation*
Commemorations may witness to past and continuing rifts and divisions within the community of faith and to the prayer that they may be overcome.

4. *Celebration*
Particular Christian communities will wish to have in remembrance those who are honoured in their locality as 'heroes' of the faith.

11

A miscellany of feasts

This chapter gathers together a number of days, rules and insights that are an important part of CLC 2000, which have not arisen naturally in looking at the cycle of the year or the commemoration of the saints.

SUNDAYS

The very first note in CLC 2000, even before mention of principal feasts, is that 'all Sundays celebrate the paschal mystery of the death and resurrection of the Lord'. It goes on to say that, 'nevertheless, they also reflect the character of the seasons in which they are set'. A calendar revised at the end of the twentieth century does well to begin with the primacy of Sunday and its special place in the week. Sunday is not simply about the need for a day of rest, but about the weekly celebration of the resurrection. It is for this reason that the rules sometimes discourage and sometimes forbid saints' days on Sundays, lest the paschal character of Sunday be lost. This book has indicated where that can be relaxed somewhat, but it should never be relaxed too much. Nor should the local church give in too often to designate a particular Sunday for a particular cause or interest group. Christian Aid, Sailors, CMS or whatever are important, but titles like 'Sea Sunday' and willingness to abandon the set prayers and lections soon undermine the character of seasons and the nature of Sunday as a 'little Easter'.

A miscellany of feasts

The second part of the note reflects the need for Sundays to go with their own seasons. Thus, for instance, though every Sunday has a paschal element, the Easter Anthems on the Sundays of Epiphany probably strike the wrong note, and cascades of alleluias on the Sundays of Lent interpret the mood quite wrongly and undermine the character of the season.

FESTIVALS OF THE LORD

Most of the days that celebrate key moments in the life of the Lord or relate to him in other ways are principal feasts and these have all been addressed. Five are festivals. Of these three – his Naming and Circumcision, his Baptism and 'Christ the King' have been discussed already. The Baptism is nearly always on a Sunday, Christ the King always so, and the Naming, though it could be transferred from Sunday to Monday, is more appropriately kept on a Sunday when it falls on that day. This leaves two festivals of the Lord.

The first is the Transfiguration on 6 August. It is, of course, a second day when that story features, for it provides the 'theme' of the Sunday next before Lent. But there is room for both, for, placed where they are in the year, they acquire very different character from one another. To read the story of the transfiguration just before Lent is to focus on its chronological place in the story of Jesus and its function as a turning point in his own ministry, coming down from the mountain and setting his face steadfastly towards Jerusalem. Coming within weeks of the Baptism it also relates those two events, united by the similar words from heaven, addressed to the Beloved Son. August 6 is different. It is somehow out of time and out of season. The key word is 'glory'. Summer sun sometimes conspires with the calendar to add to the sense of glory. But this day also has its dark side; for many 6 August is also always a day to remember the bombing of Hiroshima. There is no day on which God's power to transfigure needs to be celebrated more. Although the rules would allow, transferring Transfiguration, falling on a Sunday, to the Monday, would be odd indeed. *Enriching the Christian Year* provides a wealth of liturgical material for the day.

The other such festival has something of the same character. This is Holy Cross Day on 14 September. It has been in the Western calendar since the seventh century. The Prayer Book names it among the 'black-letter days'. *The Proposed Prayer Book* of 1928 and the ASB both gave it collect and readings, but only in CLC 2000 has it been given the status of a festival. In origin it is related to the finding of the 'true cross' by the Empress Helena and its later setting up by the Emperor Heraclius in Jerusalem in the year 629 after its recovery from the Persians. Opinion will vary on the historicity of this series of events. But that hardly matters, for what Holy Cross Day has become is an opportunity to reflect on the place of the cross in Christian life and devotion, and in particular of the glory of the cross, away from the particular mood of Holy Week and Good Friday. It is to come at the cross from a different angle and it is a creative thing to do.

CELEBRATING THE PATRON SAINT

CLC 2000 requires each church to celebrate its patron saint or its 'feast of title' (i.e. the event, mystery or aspect of the godhead after which it is named) as a festival or a principal feast. There may seem to be little difference in practice between the two, but if the day is kept as a principal feast it allows it to be celebrated in Easter

Week or a Sunday even in Advent, Lent or Easter. Thus, for instance, a church dedicated to St George could, in a year when Easter is late, still keep its patronal festival on 23 April even if it were Easter Monday, and a church dedicated to St Cuthbert, in a year when 20 March was a Sunday, could still keep its patronal festival on a Sunday in Lent. Indeed the note on 'Local Celebrations' goes further and allows the transfer of the patronal festival, when it falls on a weekday, to the nearest Sunday. The rule reads: 'When kept as principal feasts, the Patronal and Dedication Festivals may be transferred to the nearest Sunday, unless that day is already a principal feast or one of the following days: The First Sunday of Advent, The Baptism of Christ, The First Sunday in Lent, The Fifth Sunday of Lent or Palm Sunday.' These exceptions preserve the high point of the Christian year, but otherwise officially permit the kind of common sense arrangements people make to ensure the proper celebration of their patronal festival.

If the patron saint is not one among the festivals in the calendar, a set of prayers, psalms and readings for both Holy Communion and Morning and Evening Prayer has to be constructed from among the wide 'common provision'. There is no shortage of suitable material for even the rarest dedication.

THE DEDICATION FESTIVAL

The Dedication Festival itself is sometimes misunderstood. It is not to be confused with the Patronal Festival. It does not celebrate the saint or mystery to which the church is dedicated. It is, when known, the anniversary of the day on which the church was dedicated or consecrated, and, when unknown, another day designated as such, so that there may be a day to reflect on and give thanks for the place of the church building in the life of the local community and Christian fellowship. There is a strong case for not being obsessed with the building, and for being a good deal more interested in the dedication of the people than of the stones or bricks, but equally there is case, just once a year, to focus on the building and to give thanks for it. That is what the Dedication Festival is for.

When the date is unknown, as is the case with the majority of ancient churches, CLC 2000 suggests either the First Sunday in October (though sometimes people keep Harvest Thanksgiving then) or the Last Sunday after Trinity (though that can also be Bible Sunday), but allows any suitable date chosen locally. Once chosen, the day can be regarded as a principal feast, rather than a festival, and, just as with a patronal festival, this then means its possible transfer to the nearest Sunday and observance on a Sunday even in Advent, Lent or Easter. Exactly the same rules apply. *Enriching the Christian Year* provides a chapter of liturgical texts for its celebration.

HARVEST THANKSGIVING

Harvest Thanksgiving has no set date and is a matter for local decision. The rule for its celebration allows it to replace the Sunday provision, as long as it does not displace a principal feast or festival. If Harvest Thanksgiving is in late September or early October, as seems to be the case in most communities despite the fact that the harvest is normally gathered in rather earlier, this simply means avoiding St Matthew's Day and Michaelmas Day when they fall on Sundays in September.

The lectionary provides a three-year cycle of Harvest readings with some alternatives within each year's provision. Some of the readings are a good deal less 'agricultural' than others and focus more broadly on thanksgiving. Here they betray their lectionary origins, as in North American observance where 'Thanksgiving' is something wider than harvest. But there are many readings of the more traditional kind and enough to provide for Morning and Evening Prayer as well as the Holy Communion.

It should be noted that CLC 2000, like other provisions before, speaks consistently of 'Harvest Thanksgiving', rather than 'Harvest Festival', as the preferred title of the day. Thanksgiving to God is the main thrust of the celebration. Again, *Enriching the Christian Year* provides a wealth of texts.

EMBER DAYS

Ember Days are traditionally more fast than feast. Nevertheless they find a place in this chapter. Never have Ember Days been more important for the well-being of the Church. With an increasing number of people experiencing a call to some kind of ministry, and yet with a crisis in vocations to ordained stipendiary ministry, the need for prayer for vocation and ministry is vital. The Ember Days, fixed to four ordination times (two of which, Advent and Lent, are now used for ordinations infrequently), often seem to miss their mark, not least on occasions in being the week after the ordinations, rather than before. The CLC 2000 notes for the Ember Days faces these problems and encourages a more creative use of them:

> Ember Days should be kept, under the Bishop's directions, in the week before an ordination as days of prayer for those to be made deacon or priest.
>
> Ember Days may also be kept even when there is no ordination in the diocese as more general days of

prayer for those who serve the Church in its various ministries, both ordained and lay, and for vocations.

Traditionally they have been observed on the Wednesdays, Fridays and Saturdays within the weeks before the Third Sunday of Advent, the Second Sunday of Lent and the Sundays nearest 29 June and 29 September.

Whereas the ASB provided collects for Ember Days and sets of different readings for each of the four Ember Weeks, CLC 2000 prefers to provide a wider set of material for 'Ministry (including Ember Days)', collects 'for the ministry of all Christian people', 'for those to be ordained', 'for vocations' and 'for the inauguration of a new ministry', two post communion prayers, psalms and fifteen lections from which the minister may choose, and red or the colour of the season for liturgical colour. Here is sufficient flexibility to allow the Ember Days to be reinstated as significant days of prayer.

12

An alternative approach to lectionary

Lectionary Note 7 in CLC 2000 aroused some controversy. In its final authorized form it reads:

> During the period from the First Sunday of Advent to the Presentation of Christ in the Temple, during the period from Ash Wednesday to Trinity Sunday, and on All Saints' Day, the readings shall come from an authorized lectionary. During Ordinary Time (i.e. between the Presentation and Ash Wednesday and between Trinity Sunday and Advent Sunday) authorized lectionary provision remains the norm but, after due consultation with the Parochial Church Council, the Minister may, from time to time, depart from the lectionary provision for pastoral reasons or preaching or teaching purposes.

The controversy lay in the fact that, for some, this goes too far, or too far at this particular moment, whereas for others it does not introduce sufficient liberty. The Church of England has been a church in which a lectionary has been normative. Clergy have departed from lectionary provision on occasions for pastoral reasons, but not many of them have done so often. There has been an expectation that at the Holy Communion and at Morning and Evening Prayer the 'set readings' will be employed. But there are churches, probably a growing number, and among them large and successful church communities in the evangelical tradition, that have increasingly sat light to lectionary provision. Many people in such churches hardly know it exists or, if they do, imagine it is advisory, rather than mandatory.

Churches have followed that line for a variety of reasons. With some it has been a simple desire to claim a freedom, open to the Spirit's guiding, to make decisions locally. For some it has been about devising sermon courses, and often needing them to fit 'terms' rather than the seasons of the Christian year. For some it has been more about how Scripture is helpfully read and a desire to stay with a book, reading semi-continuously, rather than jumping around thematically.

The background to the present note emerges in stages. *The Promise of His Glory* first advocated an alternative lectionary approach for the part of the year that it covered and, for good measure, provided a series of carefully designed packages of scriptural material, suited to the time of year, focusing on particular books of the Bible and reading them semi-continuously. It was a desire to restore semi-continuous reading in a church that lived with a thematic (ASB) lectionary. It set limits on when the alternative material might be used; the book covered in any case only the period from 1 November to 2 February, but additionally Advent 3 to Epiphany 1 were to follow the mainstream authorized lectionaries, in order that the Church should come together around the great festivals and the central Christian mysteries.

Patterns for Worship, leading to *A Service of the Word* (authorized by the General Synod for use from 1993 to 2000), concerned with the whole Christian year and not just one quarter of it, moved the matter on. *Patterns for Worship* provided some guidelines on local lectionary compilation and *A Service of the Word* provided a clear rule (Note 5): 'The readings shall come from an authorized lectionary during the periods from Advent 3 to Epiphany 1 and from Palm Sunday to Trinity Sunday and whenever the service is combined with the Eucharist.'

Once again, there is a freedom to use alternative and locally devised material except around the great festivals, and therefore, through this rule, for nearly nine months of the year, but with a crucial constraint, that this freedom does not apply to the Holy Communion. Until the Liturgical Commission came to the General Synod with its 1995 report, there was no proposal to create a long 'open lectionary season' that included the Eucharist.

In that 1995 report the Commission argued for the lectionary year to be divided between 'closed' and 'open' seasons. The closed seasons would be those already named in the Service of the Word rule, i.e. from Advent 3 to the Baptism of Christ and Palm Sunday to Trinity Sunday. The rest of the year would constitute the open seasons, for which authorized alternative packages would be available when churches would also be free to construct their own. The Commission would in due course bring forward packages of lectionary material for commendation by the House of Bishops. There would be safeguards to ensure that opting out of the main lectionary would be occasional, rather than frequent, even in Ordinary Time, and there was a hope expressed that, since *The Revised Common Lectionary* itself reversed the move to thematic readings and restored a semi-continuous approach, few would want to go down this alternative lectionary route.

The Revision Committee believed that what the Commission had proposed was going too far. One did not commend a new lectionary, in which one was rightly confident, by allowing people to deviate from it straight away. One did not encourage the commonality of worship by imposing a lectionary for only a quarter of it. There was a fear that this was a step, if not too far, certainly too soon, and a belief that at most a more restricted 'open season' should be allowed. The Committee went back to the Synod with a recommendation to restrict the open lectionary period to Ordinary Time, to require consultation with the Parochial Church Council before any use of the alternative lectionary provision, and to remove the provision for the House of Bishops to commend alternative lectionary passages. Only a handful of people rose to support a move to refer the matter back to the Revision Committee, and so it is a much more restricted permission that has been given. It does apply at all services, including the Eucharist, but only between Candlemas and Ash Wednesday, and from after Trinity Sunday until Advent. It is a quite new freedom and allows some experiment, but it has not shifted the Church of England's position in any basic way. Reading the Scriptures together, as part of a commonality that, with the new lectionary, extends well beyond England and the Church of England, remains the ideal and the norm week by week as the Church celebrates the Christian story.

References

The Book of Alternative Services of the Anglican Church in Canada, Anglican Book Centre, Toronto, 1985.

Lent, Holy Week, Easter: Services and Prayers, Church House Publishing/Cambridge University Press/SPCK, 1996.

The Promise of His Glory: Services and Prayers for the Season of All Saints to Candlemas, Mowbray/Church House Publishing, 1991.

Celebrating Common Prayer, Mowbray, 1992.

The Revised Common Lectionary, Canterbury Press, 1992.

A Service of the Word, Church House Publishing, 1994.

Patterns for Worship, Church House Publishing, 1995.

Draper, Martin, ed. *The Cloud of Witnesses*, Alcuin Club/Collins, 1982.

Perham, Michael, ed., *The Renewal of Common Prayer*, SPCK, 1993.

Perham, Michael, ed., *Enriching the Christian Year*, SPCK, 1993.

Perham, Michael, and Stevenson, Kenneth, *Waiting for the Risen Christ*, SPCK, 1986.

Perham, Michael, and Stevenson, Kenneth, *Welcoming the Light of Christ*, SPCK, 1991.

Wilkinson, Alan, and Cocksworth, Christopher, eds, *An Anglican Companion*, SPCK/Church House Publishing, 1996.

Further reading

Dudley, Martin, 'The Lectionary', in *Towards Liturgy 2000*, Michael Perham, ed., SPCK/Alcuin Club, 1989.

Perham, Michael, 'Celebrating the Church's Year', in *Something Understood*, Paul Roberts, David Stancliffe and Kenneth Stevenson, eds, Hodder & Stoughton, 1993.

Index

Index

Index